P9-BUI-757   BOLIVAR

SIMÓN BOLÍVAR

South American Liberator

David Goodnough

Enslow Publishers, Inc.

40 Industrial Road	PO Box 38
Box 398	Aldershot
Berkeley Heights, NJ 07922	Hants GU12 6BP
USA	UK

http://www.enslow.com

Library of Congress Cataloging-in-Publication Data

Goodnough, David.
   Simón Bolívar: South American Liberator / David Goodnough
   p.   cm. — (Hispanic biographies)
   Includes bibliographical references and index.
   Summary: A biography of the South American general and revolutionary who helped liberate Bolivia, Colombia, Ecuador, Peru, and Venezuela from the domination of Spain in the early nineteenth century.
   ISBN 0-7660-1044-9
   1. Bolívar, Simón, 1783–1830—Juvenile literature. 2. Latin America—History—Wars of Independence, 1806–1830—Juvenile literature. 3. Latin American federation—Juvenile literature. 4. Heads of state—South America—Biography—Juvenile literature. [1. Bolívar, Simón, 1783–1830. 2. Heads of state. 3. South America—History—Wars of Independence, 1806–1830.] I. Title. II. Series.
   F2235.3.G832   1998
   980'.02'092—dc21
   [B]   98-23356
                                    CIP
                                    AC

Printed in the United States of America

10 9 8 7 6 5 4 3

Illustration Credits: Maryknoll Fathers Archives, pp. 7, 12, 16, 49, 73, 78, 83, 85, 86; Enslow Publishers, Inc., pp. 10, 20, 43, 89, 97; New York Public Library Picture Collection, pp. 37, 64; David Goodnough, p. 76.

Cover Illustration: New York Public Library Picture Collection

CONTENTS

CROSSING
THE ANDES

 In June 1819 a ragged army of poorly trained troops—mercenary, or hired, soldiers; foreign volunteers; freed slaves; and outlaws—did what was then thought to be impossible. They set out from Venezuela and crossed the towering Andes Mountains to invade New Granada (now Colombia), which lay between the mountain range and the Pacific Ocean to the west.

The army proceeded without maps into unknown territory, guided only by friendly Indians. They marched through the "green hell" of western

Venezuela—the swamps and rain-swollen rivers filled with alligators and flesh-eating fish. The army, including wives, girlfriends, and children of the troops, was made up mostly of people who lived in the flat plains of eastern Venezuela. They gasped in surprise and wonder at the 19,000-foot-high peaks that faced them, and some of them gave up then and there rather than continue. Those who remained managed to climb through perilous mountain passes, crossing deep chasms on dangerous rope bridges, until they finally reached the high plains of New Granada. That they were able to do so was due to the sheer will and determination of their leader, Simón Bolívar.

The Andes of South America have the highest peaks and plains of any mountain range in the Western Hemisphere. They stretch from Chile in the far south to Venezuela and Colombia in the north and contain some of the wildest and most rugged country in the world. In the early part of the nineteenth century, they were still being challenged by explorers and traders who sought to find an easy route across them. They were inhabited by the few native peoples who had lived there long before and after the Spanish conquest of the Incan and Mayan empires of Peru and Mexico, more than two hundred years before.

The army was led by General Simón Bolívar, president of the newly formed republic of Venezuela. His own country was now free from the oppressive

A church in the Andes Mountains of present-day Colombia, South America. These are the high plains in which Bolívar defeated the Spanish Army in his invasion of New Granada.

Spanish rule that had begun three hundred years ago, when Spain had colonized almost all of South America. He fought in the revolutions beginning in 1810 that returned his country to the Spanish-speaking colonists who had been born there. They had also liberated the Indians and freed slaves who had been used by Spain to mine and cultivate the rich natural resources of the continent.

Now that his own country was freed, Bolívar turned his attention to the neighboring province of New Granada to continue his goal of freeing all of Spanish America from Spain.

Bolívar chose the most difficult route across the Andes to avoid the superior Spanish forces who guarded the obvious crossing places. His army began its climb during the rainy season, when the steep ground was wet and slippery. The troops had only light clothing, and as they approached the snow line, many died from the cold. Others were affected by the soroche, a sickness caused by the high altitude and thin air, producing nausea and sleeplessness that could result in injury or even death. The army crossed rushing mountain streams, where much of their equipment and most of their horses were lost. They built frail bridges over deep chasms, and slogged through the mud and ice of twelve-thousand-foot-high pastures and passes. By the time they reached the high plains leading to the capital city of Bogotá, Bolívar had lost a third of his army.

When the exhausted army finally arrived on the high plains of New Granada, many of the soldiers swore that they would die in battle rather than recross the mountains. Although the Spanish were surprised when Bolívar's army appeared, they were quick to block the main roads and bridges leading to the capital. Again, Bolívar chose the most difficult route and led his exhausted men across the open plain of Pisba, which was considered impassable in the rainy season.

When they arrived at the valley of the Sogamosa River, nine thousand feet above sea level, the army was in poor condition. Many of the soldiers had lost their weapons and had thrown away their food rations to lighten their loads. The cavalry had lost most of its horses, and the *llaneros*, the hard-riding cowboys of Venezuela, were not used to fighting on foot.

In the days that followed, the army fought a few skirmishes and small battles during which they managed to win or at least succeeded in holding off the enemy. Bolívar rallied his men time and time again. His opponents, the Spanish, were indecisive and their troops were unreliable. Bolívar's army was saved from destruction by the courage of his British soldiers, who were loyal to him even though they had been paid to join his forces. He was also aided by the fierceness of

South America

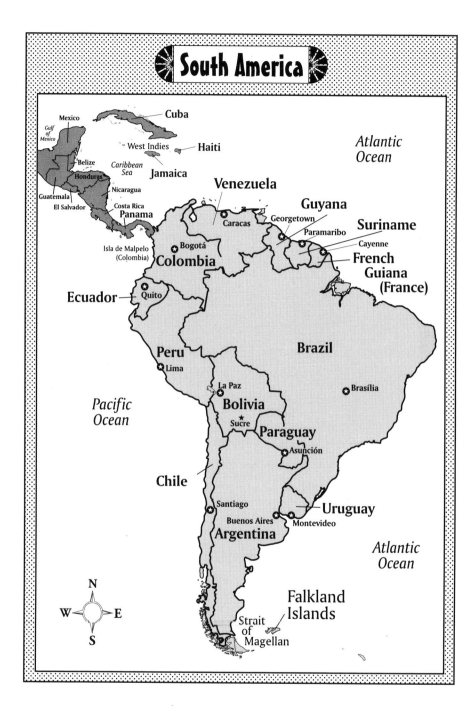

Mexico
Gulf of Mexico
Cuba
West Indies
Haiti
Belize
Caribbean Sea
Jamaica
Honduras
Guatemala
Nicaragua
El Salvador
Costa Rica
Panama
Atlantic Ocean

Isla de Malpelo (Colombia)
Bogotá
Colombia
Ecuador
Quito

Venezuela
Caracas
Guyana
Georgetown
Paramaribo
Suriname
Cayenne
French Guiana (France)

Peru
Lima
La Paz
Bolivia
Sucre
Brazil
Brasília

Pacific Ocean

Paraguay
Asunción

Chile
Santiago
Buenos Aires
Argentina
Montevideo
Uruguay

Atlantic Ocean

N
W E
S

Falkland Islands
Strait of Magellan

Map of South America

the llaneros, who charged the Spanish lines on the few horses they had left.

Most of the men in the Spanish forces were Granadinos, born in Spanish America rather than Spain, so their loyalties were divided. Bolívar had little trouble convincing the soldiers he captured to join his army, and he also recruited all able-bodied men and boys from the towns he passed through.

His main objective was the city of Bogotá, and the shortest way there was over the bridge at Boyacá, northeast of the city. The Spanish commander, making a slow withdrawal to Bogotá, found himself nearly surrounded at the bridge. Bolívar had made a quick march of his army at night and had completely surprised the Spanish. The Battle of Boyacá on August 7, 1819, was actually little more than a skirmish, but it marked the final defeat of the Spanish forces. Most of the soldiers who surrendered at Boyacá were Venezuelans who had been drafted into the Spanish Army, so Bolívar merely added them to his own army. There was now nothing standing in his way to the capital city of Bogotá.

On August 10, Bolívar learned that the viceroy, or governor, of New Granada, Juan Sámano, had fled Bogotá. Sámano was a cruel and ruthless tyrant who was despised by the people of New Granada. He knew that he could expect no mercy from his conquerors, and he left the city in such a hurry that he neglected to

BO
QUE ASEG
GRANAD

BOLIVAR

Memorial to the Battle of Boyacá, which was fought in 1819, in present-day Colombia, South America.

take the country's treasury with him.[1] Bolívar rushed to Bogotá and took possession of the city, but he did not make his formal entry until September 18, 1819. He now had enough money from the captured treasury to pay his soldiers. He also gave them a long rest and time to ready themselves for their official entry into the capital city.

When the great day arrived, the streets and balconies of buildings were filled with people who threw flowers and shouted praises as Bolívar led his proud troops to the great square in front of the cathedral. All the church bells in the city pealed loudly as Bolívar, his officers, and government officials entered the cathedral where they knelt to give thanks for their victory. After listening to a Latin hymn of thanksgiving, they returned to the square outside where a special platform had been built for Bolívar and his company. It was shaded by a rich cloth cover and decorated with six statues representing the virtues of the hero. A hymn especially composed in his honor was sung by a choir, and a young maiden, clad in all white, crowned him with a wreath of laurel. Bolívar took it off and gestured with it toward his troops lined up in the square. "Those soldiers are the men who deserve it," he shouted, and threw the crown to them.[2] The crowd went wild.

Simón Bolívar was then only thirty-six years old. This was his third attempt to expel the Spanish from

Spanish America. In this hour of his greatest success, it must have seemed to him that he was destined to achieve his goal. His dream was to unify all the separate provinces of Spanish America into one unified country like the United States. He nearly did it.

THE CREOLE
MILLIONAIRE

Simón Bolívar was born in Caracas, Venezuela, on July 24, 1783, to a wealthy Creole family. Creoles are people of Spanish descent who had been born in Spanish America. Simón's family was one of the oldest Creole families in Venezuela. The Bolívars had been in South America since the early days of the Spanish exploration and conquest, more than two hundred years earlier. They held vast estates and owned slaves, and they had some influence in the affairs of the country.

Venezuela was then a part of the viceroyalty of New Granada, and the government was headed by a viceroy who owed his allegiance to Charles IV, the king of Spain. Although the Creoles owned and worked the land and sent most of its natural resources to Spain, they were heavily taxed and had little say in their own government. Even such important people as the Bolívars were denied any high government posts.

Simón's father, a big spender and a playboy, never had much contact with his son. The family's estates were managed by his stern mother, who had little time for her son. Like most wealthy Creole children, Simón was cared for by nurses and housekeepers, who were usually slaves. Simón's nurse was a slave named Hipólita, who he said later was his only true mother.[1] Both his parents died when he was young, and at the

Caracas is the capital of Venezuela and the birthplace of Simón Bolívar.

age of seven he was turned over to tutors for the rest of his upbringing and education. One of these tutors was the radical Simón Rodríguez.

Rodríguez was only twenty years old, but he had already traveled throughout Europe, where he had been a philosophy student. He had also managed to get himself into trouble by preaching radical ideas in public. He was an enthusiastic follower of the ideas of the French philosopher Jean-Jacques Rousseau, who believed that all government and social customs burdened rather than helped people in their development. In Simón, Rodríguez found someone who was loud and fun-loving and preferred horseback riding and dancing to schoolwork. Simón loved to read, but he usually read what he wanted to rather than what he was expected to read as a student. Rodríguez and Simón rode and hunted together on the Bolívars' lands.

Rodríguez was also a revolutionary, and New Granada as well as the rest of Spanish South America had been burning with revolutionary feeling for a long time. The main cause of the people's discontent was the old story of taxation without representation, which had led the North American colonies to revolt against England in 1775. Another was the strict control that Spain held over trade. There had been many attempts by dissatisfied groups to overthrow the Spanish rulers of their country, but all had failed. The trouble was that these uprisings came from groups that did not represent all of the people.

The society of the Spanish colonies in South America was composed of five different classes of people. First were the Spanish officials sent out from Spain to govern the colonies. Their purpose was to maintain law and order and to assure that the raw materials and riches of the new lands were sent to Spain. Along the way they managed to enrich themselves as well as Spain, and many of them were corrupt and cruel in their pursuit of personal wealth. Next came the Creoles, Spaniards who had been born in the colonies but still owed their allegiance to Spain. These were the landowners and merchants who supplied Spain with most of its wealth, but keeping as much as they could for themselves. The third class were *mestizos*, or people of mixed European and Indian blood. These were mostly farmers and laborers who were employed by the Creoles. Next came the African slaves and people of mixed African, Indian, or European descent, called *castas* by the Creoles. Many of them were freedmen, not slaves, but were still considered little more than slaves. The fifth class were the native Indians, who if they were considered at all were treated as slave labor. The government had no interest in them except to keep them in their place and not to let them interfere with the functions of colonial society.

All of these groups were interested mostly in themselves and their own affairs, so there was little unity among them. Whenever one group or class rebelled against the injustices of the colonial system, the others either ignored them or joined the government in putting them down. If the slaves revolted, the Creoles and mestizos would unite with the Spanish to defeat them, since they were a threat to all of them. If the Creoles demanded independent rights, especially in trade, the mestizos and the slaves or freed slaves refused to join them, since they had nothing to gain from foreign trade.

In 1797, Rodríguez became involved in a plot by two Creole intellectuals to overthrow the government. The leaders were betrayed by an informer, and the government moved swiftly to crush the revolt. Rodríguez escaped punishment but was kept under close watch by the authorities. Even that was too much for a free spirit like Rodríguez, and he left Venezuela aboard a British ship.[2]

By the time Rodríguez left, Simón was fourteen years old. He joined a cadet corps that had been organized many years before by his father, but he did not receive much military training. He enjoyed the horseback riding and the parades and dressing up in a fancy uniform but was too restless for discipline. He rose to the rank of lieutenant, mainly because of his family's connections. He spent most of his time dancing, which he loved, and riding, swimming, and dueling, all of which he did well. His family began to worry about his lack of direction and decided to send him to Spain to learn manners and refinement in the royal court.

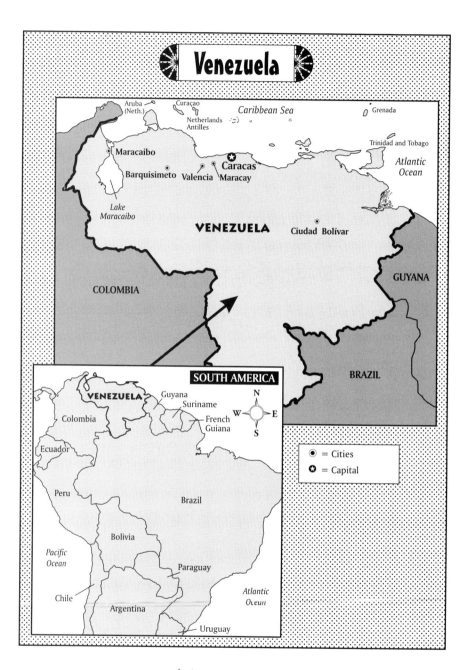

Map of Venezuela

Because he was wealthy and came from one of the finest Creole families, he could be assured of coming into contact with the best that Spain had to offer a young man from the colonies.

Simón arrived in Spain in the spring of 1799, after a short stay in Mexico. He was sixteen years old, intelligent, handsome, and rich. He was soon caught up in the social whirl of the capital and was invited to the best homes and introduced to the most important and powerful people. King Charles IV and his wife, María Luisa, presided over a court that was infamous throughout Europe for its loose living. None of this escaped Simón, who was invited to court and was able to observe the activities of the royal family. Prince Ferdinand, the king's eldest son, who was one day to become king of Spain, was only two years older than Simón.

One day the prince, who was a vain and conceited young man, challenged Simón to a game of racquetball. The prince expected to win, if not by skill then by his right as a prince. Simón, however, was an excellent player and had no intention of letting the prince win just because he was a member of the royal family. As the game progressed, Simón drove the ball so hard that it knocked the prince's hat off his head. The prince expected an apology, but Simón did not offer any.[3]

Simón became well known in Madrid, and everyone wanted to know the handsome young man who could fight and ride as well as he could dance and play cards all night. He was invited to the grandest houses and entertained by all the noble families of Madrid. He was constantly thrown together with young ladies of his own age.

It was not long before he fell in love with the quiet and charming María Teresa de Toro. She too had been born in Caracas into a wealthy and cultured Creole family, who had left Venezuela and settled in Spain. The de Toros preferred the elegance and refinement of Spanish society to that of Venezuela, so they were not entirely pleased when the dashing and rather wild young man from Caracas respectfully asked for María Teresa's hand in marriage.

María Teresa was almost two years older than Simón, and the cautious de Toros thought that the seventeen-year-old Simón was not ready to be a husband. María Teresa's father suggested that Simón take a year off to travel. If at the end of the year, Simón still wanted to marry, he would have the family's consent. Simón, who never doubted the power and sincerity of his love for María Teresa, readily agreed. In 1801 he set out for Paris, France, more anxious to fulfill his commitment to María Teresa than to observe the wide world.

At the time of Simón's journey to France, Napoleon Bonaparte was at the head of the revolutionary government as first consul. Simón admired him greatly, for here was a common soldier who had achieved command of a great country through ability alone and not through heredity or position. One of Napoleon's greatest accomplishments was the establishment of law codes. These codes included religious tolerance and the end of serfdom. All of this contrasted strongly with the conditions Simón was familiar with in Venezuela. His admiration for Napoleon and his works did not inspire any revolutionary thoughts in Simón, however. He was very much in love and desired nothing more than to return to Spain and claim his bride.

Simón's year of separation from María Teresa finally ended, and he returned eagerly to Spain. He and María Teresa were married in Madrid on May 26, 1802, and they quickly left for Venezuela. When he arrived home, Simón took his wife to one of his family's estates outside Caracas. There they led a leisurely life away from the distractions of government and society. He devoted himself completely to his wife and let others worry about the state of the world in general and of Venezuela in particular. It was the happiest time of his young life.[4]

The young couple were married only ten months when disaster struck. In January 1903, María Teresa suddenly became ill. Five days later she was dead from a tropical fever. Bolívar was crushed. His happiness had ended practically as soon as it had begun. He was a widower at the age of twenty, and he vowed that he would never marry again. Life in the large house and in Venezuela became meaningless. He decided to return to Europe.

THE YOUNG
REVOLUTIONARY

Bolívar returned to Madrid in 1804. However, the city brought back memories of María Teresa, and his aristocratic friends began to bore him. He was also rudely reminded that he was, after all, a Creole from the colonies. At that time there was a wave of distrust of foreigners in Spain, and the government began to expel them. The excuse used was that there was a food shortage, and Spain could not afford to shelter people who did not live there. When it was suggested that Bolívar leave, he gladly departed for Paris, never again to return to Spain.

Paris was still considered the capital city of Europe. Although he had many friends among the nobility, Bolívar became acquainted with many serious thinkers. These thinkers were familiar with the modern political ideas of democracy and freedom of thought. A distant cousin of his, Fanny du Villars, was known for her parties that attracted the artists, writers, and philosophers of France. Bolívar often attended these gatherings and there met the famous German explorer and scientist Alexander von Humboldt. Humboldt had spent some time in Venezuela and had written about it, so he and Bolívar had much to talk about. Humboldt knew about the current situation in Venezuela, and one day he said that Venezuela was ready for an independence movement against Spain. Bolívar may have heard such an opinion before, but coming from the distinguished Humboldt, it impressed him strongly. Something else that Humboldt said may have impressed him even more. "But," Humboldt said, still speaking of Venezuela's independence, "I cannot see the man who is to achieve it."[1]

It is not known whether Humboldt's remark planted the seed in the mind of Bolívar, but soon afterward he began to change. He slowly withdrew from the nightly socializing that had filled his early days in Paris. Although Bolívar had originally admired Napoleon, now Napoleon had become a virtual dictator and was planning to have himself crowned emperor of France. He still admired Napoleon's gifts as a soldier, but Bolívar later said: "I regarded him as a hypocritical tyrant."[2] So Napoleon was not only an inspiration but also a disappointment and a warning to the young man.

In 1804, Napoleon finally declared himself emperor of France and its colonies. Bolívar felt betrayed by the man he had once admired. During this period, Bolívar met his former tutor, Simón Rodríguez, who had been living in Vienna, Austria. He was as concerned about Napoleon's dictatorship in France as Bolívar was. Rodríguez suggested that they go to Italy where they could renew their friendship. In Milan, Italy, they witnessed the second coronation of Napoleon, performed for the citizens of this part of his empire. Bolívar's anger had cooled by then, although he continued to speak out against the emperor.

When they arrived in Rome, Bolívar was struck by the beauty of the city and by the traditions it represented. The people of Rome had fought against tyranny and oppression for more than two thousand years. Although they had been conquered many times, and had been ruled by tyrants as well as heroes, they still remained independent and firm in defending their right to freedom. On the Aventine Hill, overlooking the whole of ancient and modern Rome, Bolívar came to a turning point in his life and a vision of his future. He said to Rodríguez: "I swear before you, by the God of my fathers and the honor of my country: I will not rest, not in body or soul, till I have broken the chains of Spain."[3]

Bolívar left Rodriguez in Rome and returned to Paris, but he did not return to his frivolous ways. He was now twenty-three years old. At heart, he was a revolutionary, and he soon learned of an event in his homeland that stirred him to action.

In 1806, the same year that Bolívar returned to Paris, a famous old Venezuelan soldier and revolutionary had attempted to lead a rebellion against Spain. The soldier's name was Francisco de Miranda, who all his life had dreamed of an independent Venezuela. He had served as an officer in the Spanish Army, but his radical views and his hatred of Spain had soon gotten him into trouble. He had been forced to leave the country to escape arrest.

Miranda traveled throughout Europe, offering his services to anyone who would give him some base from which to continue his efforts to free his country. He fought in the French Revolution and achieved the rank of general. He served in the Russian Army of Catherine the Great. He was a brilliant fighter but often quarreled with his commanders and was forced to either resign or leave the country. For a time he was employed by William Pitt the Younger, the prime minister of England, as a spy for the English foreign office. Everywhere he went he tried to gain support and money for a revolution in Venezuela. He finally ended up in New York, where he managed to put together an army of about two hundred mercenary soldiers of different nationalities.

In February 1806, Miranda set sail with his army in three ships bound for Venezuela. The Spanish Navy had plenty of warning, and his invasion fleet was intercepted off the coast of Venezuela. Two of his ships were sunk and most of his men were captured. Miranda made his way to the United States and immediately began plans for another invasion. He borrowed more funds from American sympathizers and found more men and another ship. Six months after his first attempt, he invaded Venezuela at the small port of Coro. Instead of being greeted as a liberator, Miranda was deserted or ignored by the local population. Nevertheless, he ran up a new flag and declared that Venezuela was now a republic with him as its head. When he learned that there was a reward for his capture and that a Spanish force was on its way to Coro, Miranda wisely left the country, this time for London.

When Bolívar learned of Miranda's attempt to gain independence for his country, he immediately left for Venezuela and arrived there in early 1807. He resumed his life as a country gentleman. He had met the king and prince of Spain. He had lived in Paris and Rome and had witnessed Napoleon's coronation. He had studied and read widely under the guidance of

Rodríguez. His radical and revolutionary opinions soon became well known. At one important gathering at the governor's palace in Caracas, he was asked to propose a toast, and he agreed by raising his glass "to the freedom of Venezuela and all of America."[4] Shortly after, the captain-general of Caracas asked Bolívar to stop holding gatherings of so many young men.[5] It was rumored that he was forming an underground movement among his many friends.

Bolívar, unlike Miranda, was prepared to wait until he had built some support among the Creoles. However, in 1808, events in Europe opened the door for action sooner than expected.

Napoleon, after crowning himself emperor of France, had set out to enlarge his empire. He had conquered Italy and Austria and had become president of the Confederation of the Rhine, which meant that he controlled all of central Europe. In 1808 he invaded the Spanish peninsula and forced King Charles into giving up his throne. Napoleon made his brother, Joseph, king. However, the Spanish people revolted and declared that King Charles's son was now their rightful king. The revolt was soon crushed by the powerful French Army, and on May 3, 1808, hundreds of innocent civilians were executed. The date has become famous in Spanish history and is still remembered as a day of mourning. The Spanish refused to surrender, however, and *juntas*, or local councils, sprang up throughout the country. England, which was then at war with France, came to their aid and landed an army in Portugal and Spain. The juntas claimed to be subjects of the new king, Ferdinand VII, Bolívar's old racquetball opponent. They also claimed that, as representatives of the king, they still had control over their New World colonies. The French claimed that they ruled the colonies. As for the colonists themselves, the time was ripe for revolt, and Bolívar and his friends were ready for it.

The Spanish officials in Caracas and the other colonial capitals took their orders from the new French government in Madrid. The Creoles, the landowners and businessmen of the colonies, supported Ferdinand VII. Juntas were established throughout Spanish America that were in direct opposition to the conservative colonial government that took its orders from Spain. Bolívar did not openly break with this government, but he continued to act secretly in support of independence. He was on good terms with the new governor and captain-general, Vincente de Emparán, but he knew that sooner or later his support of independence would become known to Emparán's spy system. In the closely knit world of Caracas, it was hard to keep anything secret for long.

In Spain, the political situation became worse as Napoleon's army began to find and destroy the juntas. Bolívar and his friends decided that the time to act had come. On April 19, 1810, a group of rebels appeared before Emparán and said that since the government in Spain had weakened, it was time to establish a new and independent government in Caracas. Instead of pointing out to them that the government he represented, that of Joseph Bonaparte, had not weakened, he hesitated. Since it was a religious holiday, Holy Thursday, he suggested that first they all go to services at the cathedral.

After the services at the cathedral, Emparán agreed to go with the rebel group to the government's council chamber. There he was told that he would have to step down as governor of Venezuela. Emparán declared that he would let the people decide whether or not he should give up his position. They walked to the balcony, and one of the rebels addressed the crowd and asked if they wanted the governor to remain. The crowd, which was filled with friends of the rebels, shouted "No!" Spain's absolute rule over South America was ended and a cruel civil war begun.[6]

HIS FIRST BATTLE

The overthrow of the Spanish colonial government in 1810 was not accompanied by violence or executions or the seizing of property. The junta was enlarged to include middle-class military and professional men such as doctors and lawyers. Emparán and most of the Spanish authorities were asked to leave the country. Restrictions on trade were done away with. Indians were no longer required to pay taxes. The slave trade was eventually ended in South America, although it continued in the Caribbean colonies. The junta claimed loyalty to Ferdinand VII, and it began to reorganize the government into a representative republic based on the model of the United States. The rest of Central and South America, except for Peru and Guatemala, followed Venezuela's lead and declared its loyalty to Ferdinand VII.

The new governments immediately sought to gain recognition from the European nations and sent ambassadors there to seek aid and support. Bolívar, who had not taken an active part in the revolution, nevertheless, stood out as one of the most important, experienced, and intelligent men of the new order. He was chosen by Venezuela to go to England to plead the cause of the new nation. Because he was also rich, he could afford to pay for the entertaining and gifts that were expected of an ambassador. He was politely received in England, but because the British were allied with Spain against France, his mission did not succeed. Bolívar wanted complete independence from Spain for Venezuela, and the British thought they could not offend their ally by approving such a complete break by one of its colonies.

Francisco de Miranda was still in England, where he had gone into exile four years earlier. He was writing and making speeches for an independent Venezuela but had generally been ignored and was considered something of a nuisance by the English. Bolívar, however, knew how popular and respected Miranda was to the rest of the world, and he thought by linking himself with Miranda he would gain recognition and respect for his ideas. Bolívar asked Miranda to return to Venezuela with him, and Miranda agreed immediately.

Miranda was greeted as a hero when he arrived in Caracas on December 12, 1810, but his presence did not cause any popular uprising for independence. He was made a general in the Venezuelan Army, but since there was hardly any army to speak of, he had little real power. He wholeheartedly backed his young friend, however, and he and Bolívar increased their efforts for independence. Bolívar's underground party was now called the Patriotic Society and held public meetings in which passionate speeches were made in favor of Venezuela's independence.

On April 19, 1811, the first anniversary of the removal of the Spanish governor, there were demonstrations and meetings in Caracas, and the crowds pulled down the statue of Ferdinand VII. The junta finally gave in, and on July 5 declared the independence of Venezuela from all parties in Spain—King Joseph Bonaparte, King Ferdinand VII, and the Spanish juntas.

The reaction from Spain was swift. A Spanish admiral, Juan Domingo Monteverde, was sent with troops to restore the colonial government. Miranda was put in command of the Venezuelan forces and thought that he could use all of the resources and wealth of Venezuela.[1] The Creoles thought otherwise. Although Bolívar never failed to answer Miranda's call when it came to military duty, the relationship between the two men began to cool.

After the declaration of independence, some of the Venezuelan provinces thought they should be made separate states, and Miranda was called to put down some minor rebellions against the new government. In one such clash, in Valencia, Miranda crushed the uprising cruelly and had prisoners beheaded, placing their heads on poles to be shown throughout the province. Throughout this period, Bolívar spent much of his time alone on one of his estates. He left the day-to-day problems of command to Miranda.

When Admiral Monteverde took over command of all the Spanish forces in Venezuela, he began a relentless campaign against Miranda. He was as cruel a commander as Miranda and ordered his men to burn villages, destroy supplies, and kill anyone who showed any signs of siding with the Venezuelans. Many Creoles and farmers had never accepted the new government, and they joined in support of Monteverde.

The situation was beginning to look bad for the Venezuelans when on March 26, 1812, a great earthquake struck the whole coast of northwestern South America. It was "one of the biggest and most terrifying ever seen on earth," wrote the Spanish historian Francisco José Heredia, who was an eyewitness.[2] In

Caracas, churches and cathedrals crumbled into dust, burying all inside. Ironically, it was Holy Thursday, the third anniversary of the expulsion of Governor Emparán, and the churches were crowded. This fact, writes Heredia, "filled the common people with terror . . . for they looked upon it as a punishment for that twofold crime" of profaning the holy day and sinning against the king three years before.[3] More than ten thousand people lost their lives in Caracas alone.

The church, which had always been against the revolution, called the earthquake an "act of God" condemning the people for their treason against their king. It was noted that the royalist forces, who were encamped outside the cities, had not suffered at all.

In the middle of all this destruction, Bolívar appeared in shirtsleeves at the top of one of the heaps of rubble amid the ruins of buildings. In answer to the cries of the priests that divine justice was being dealt to the revolutionaries, Bolívar shouted, "If nature opposes us, we shall fight against her and force her to obey us."[4] The square was filled with people, and his was the only voice raised in hope and confidence. He seemed to be the only person willing to press on against what seemed to be a devastating defeat at the hands of fate.

During the confusion that followed the earthquake, the Spanish commander Monteverde continued to win victory after victory over the government forces.

Simón Bolívar after achieving success on the battlefield. This is the type of elaborate uniform that he favored for the rest of his life.

Bolívar was tireless in rallying the discouraged and disheartened army against the Spanish. But the government in Caracas made Miranda the Commander in Chief of all of Venezuela, which meant that he was its dictator. Miranda could not have helped noticing that Bolívar was his only rival in popularity and trust among the people. He was one of the few of Miranda's officers who displayed confidence and energy in the face of the enemy. Either in recognition of Bolívar's abilities or in distrust of his ambitions, Miranda appointed him commander of the fort at Puerto Cabello. By doing so, he removed Bolívar from the center of activity in Caracas.

Puerto Cabello was one of Venezuela's most important seaports. It was the entering point for most of Venezuela's supplies from Europe and the landing place for friendly foreign troops. Bolívar was a cavalry officer with little experience or training in defending a major city. He could lead a charge or rally his troops, but waiting out a siege or holding a fixed position was something he knew very little about. When Monteverde's troops attacked the city, a Venezuelan officer allowed them to take over the castle of San Filipe overlooking the city. From there the invaders fired down on the defenders of the city. Bolívar pleaded to Miranda for help, but Miranda did nothing, and the city fell to Monteverde's army.

Bolívar and his staff managed to escape by sea. The effect of this defeat on Bolívar was devastating. He had failed in a very important assignment, but he felt that his honor was intact.[5] He had been betrayed, and when he sought assistance, none had come. The gap between him and Miranda widened.

Although Monteverde had a string of successes in his campaign to regain Venezuela for Spain, he was actually in a poor position. He was outnumbered, his troops were not particularly reliable, and he did not have a firm base of supply. Miranda, however, did not take advantage of this. He continued to train and parade his men, trying to make them into a model European-style army. They were not, however, professional soldiers and did not like Miranda's strict discipline. Many of them deserted to join Monteverde. The situation became hopeless for Miranda. He began secret negotiations with Monteverde for surrender, while at the same time preparing to leave the country by sea. Shortly before surrendering his army, Miranda accepted a large payment in gold from the Spanish and ordered that a ship be made ready for his escape.

On July 11, 1812, Miranda surrendered to Monteverde and slipped out of Caracas, ready to leave the country. Bolívar was furious when he heard of the surrender, and he and a few friends intercepted Miranda before he could board his ship. They arrested him as a traitor and turned him over to the Spanish authorities, who had taken control of the capital and the seaports of Venezuela. Apparently, Monteverde thought that Bolívar's betrayal of Miranda was worthy of reward. Instead of making him a prisoner of war, he granted Bolívar free passage out of Venezuela. Bolívar left for Curaçao, an island in the Caribbean Sea. He intended to leave from there to join the army of the English general the Duke of Wellington who was fighting against Napoleon in Spain.

Miranda was imprisoned and eventually sent to Spain, where he spent the rest of his life in jail. Without Miranda's efforts, however, Bolívar's later successes would not have been possible. For this reason Miranda is known as The Precursor, or forerunner, of Bolívar, who was soon to become known as The Liberator.[6]

FIRST VICTORIES— AND DEFEAT

When Monteverde accepted Miranda's surrender in 1812, he had promised that no reprisals would be taken against the rebels and that their institutions and laws would remain. However, once he gained control of the country, he broke all his promises and became its dictator. He arrested everyone who was suspected of being a rebel. The constitution of the new republic was burned in a public ceremony, and all the members of the congress were sent to prison in Spain. In addition, Monteverde had his soldiers seize the property of wealthy Creoles and sent most of them to prison as suspected rebels. When Bolívar heard of all this—especially of the seizure of his property—he abandoned his plans to leave for Europe. From then on, he devoted himself completely to ridding his country of Monteverde and continuing his personal war against Spain.

The neighboring province of New Granada, which was made up of what is now Colombia, Panama, and Ecuador, had successfully rebelled against Spain. Now that Venezuela's revolution had failed, New Granada was faced once again with hostile Spanish forces just across its borders. New Granada was not a unified country ready to repel invaders. Some parts had declared themselves independent, while others were still trying to decide what to do with their new freedom. Bolívar saw this as an opportunity to continue his fight against Spain and to rebuild his reputation as a soldier and a leader. In October 1812 he journeyed to the independent city of Cartagena on the northwestern coast of what is now Colombia and offered the city officials his advice and help.

Bolívar was not yet thirty years old, but he had seen and learned much. He now felt prepared to lead an army and saw the opportunity to do so in New Granada. The government of Cartagena accepted Bolívar's offer of help and made him a full colonel. Bolívar immediately began to plan an invasion of Venezuela. It seemed to the government leaders an

Colombia

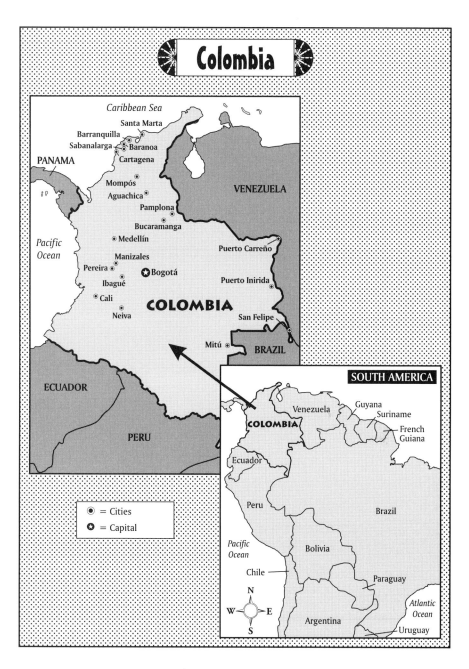

Map of Colombia

ambitious and perhaps risky undertaking, and they were not quite ready for it. They sent Bolívar to command a small army post in Barrancas on the banks of the Magdalena River.

Before leaving for Barrancas, Bolívar wrote open letters to the people of Cartagena that were published in the local newspapers. These letters were collected in a pamphlet, which became known as the Cartagena Manifesto. In it Bolívar summarized the recent history of Venezuela and warned that the same thing could happen to New Granada. He urged the people to unite under a strong central government that could present a unified front against the Spanish forces.[1]

The Magdalena River lay northeast of Cartagena and was occupied on one of its banks by Spanish forces. The Commander in Chief of the Cartagena forces was a French soldier named Labatud or Labatut. Preparing an attack on the Spanish forces at the port of Santa Marta farther to the east, he instructed Bolívar merely to hold his position on the river. Bolívar, however, was not about to let a Frenchman have an easy victory while he sat idle on the banks of the Magdalena. He rallied the two hundred men under his command and floated upriver on barges to attack the Spanish fort at Tenerife. His maneuver was so swift and unexpected that the Spanish fled the fort, leaving their supplies behind. Bolívar then quickly moved his men upriver to the next town, Mompox. There he was openly greeted by the people and recruited three hundred additional men for his army.

Labatud protested bitterly to the government of Cartagena that Bolívar had disobeyed orders and that he should be court-martialed. But the officials in Cartagena were not going to argue against success, especially when it was brought about by a popular Creole officer. It was clear to them that here at last was a man who could command with authority and make crucial decisions on his own. Bolívar was rewarded for his victories with a promotion to military commander of the area he had regained from the Spanish. In addition, he was given some more men and supplies. This was the first victory of his career, and he realized its importance. "I was born in Caracas," he said, "but my fame was born in Mompox."[2]

Once again, Bolívar did not allow his troops to rest. He won five more victories in less than a week and cleared the whole river of Spanish forces. He then marched overland and cleared the whole province of Santa Marta, which bordered Venezuela. It was now clear that not only was Bolívar an exceptional soldier, but that the Spanish were not all that powerful. Bolívar's argument for an invasion of Venezuela suddenly began to make sense to the government at Cartagena. Bolívar was promoted to brigadier general and was given permission to plan and carry out an attack on Caracas.

Bolívar had been made an honorary citizen of New Granada, but he was still considered a foreigner by many of his men and most of his officers. They felt that the most important thing to do was to hold their own country against any Spanish counterattacks. They did not want to run off to free somebody else's country.

Monteverde, meantime, had set up a chain of defenses stretching from the sea in the north to the passes in the Andes Mountains to the south. Bolívar knew that it was merely a matter of time before the Spanish forces were reinforced from the sea and that they could strike anywhere along the coast, outflanking his meager land forces. He therefore had to strike quickly, which was a difficult matter, considering the types of soldiers he had. They were mostly poor, undertrained, and underpaid—if they were paid at all—unskilled laborers from the lower classes. Mixed in with them were mercenaries and criminals. The one thing they held against Bolívar was that he did not give them time to loot the territories they took from the Spanish. All too often, after a victory, they were regrouped and sent off on another campaign. This left the camp followers and local bandits or neighboring townspeople to reap the rewards of their victory. Rallying them for a wholesale assault on a neighboring country took all of Bolívar's skills of persuasion.

The head of the Granadino forces under Bolívar's command was Colonel Manuel Castillo. Castillo urged caution in advancing against the Spanish. He wished to consolidate the gains already made and remain within his own country in case his men were needed to put down the many internal revolts that still plagued the new republic. Bolívar felt that the only way to protect New Granada was to regain Venezuela, and he and Castillo became outright opponents over this matter. Castillo scored a victory when he took control of the pass through the Andes at La Grita. The Spanish forces were forced to retreat into Venezuela, and the way was open to the Venezuelan lowlands. It was here that Castillo halted and, in Bolívar's absence, called a council of war in which he declared he would advance no farther. When objections were raised, he resigned his command.

Bolívar rushed to La Grita and took charge. The officer who succeeded Castillo was Francisco de Paula Santander, a young officer who was as ambitious as Bolívar. When Bolívar arrived in La Grita, he ordered Santander to advance his army as it had been ordered to do while under the command of Castillo. Santander refused. Bolívar drew his pistol and said, "March! There is no alternative. Either you shoot me or I shoot you."[3] Santander backed off, and he was later dismissed as head of the Granadino forces, but he never forgot the episode. He and Bolívar were to meet, serve together, and confront each other again and again over the years.

Bolívar insisted on speed in the invasion of Venezuela for another reason. In the eastern part of the country the invasion of the province had already begun under the leadership of Santiago Mariño. Mariño was a Venezuelan officer who fled to Trinidad, an island off the coast of Venezuela, after Miranda's surrender to Monteverde. With the aid of the English in Trinidad, Mariño won steadily against the unprepared Spanish forces. Monteverde, besides being a very poor general, made matters worse by encouraging his troops to loot and destroy anything that they came across while advancing or even retreating. The people were turning against Monteverde, and Mariño was advancing rapidly on Caracas. To Bolívar, who saw himself as the only true liberator of his country, it was absolutely vital that he be the first to enter Caracas as the conquering hero.

One of the least admirable tactics that Bolívar used to speed his campaign and demoralize his opponents was to instill terror in his enemies, both military and civilian. While Bolívar and Castillo were arguing over the invasion, they were given a plan known as the War to the Death Plan.[4] It stated that "the first and chief aim [is] to destroy in Venezuela the accursed race of European Spaniards. . . . Not a single one must remain alive." It also provided that "the presentation of heads of European Spaniards . . . [is] sufficient to deserve reward and a commission in the army." It goes on to list how many heads it would take to become an ensign (twenty), or a lieutenant (thirty), and so on.[5]

This was an unprecedented plan. Up to that time, individual commanders had allowed their troops to loot, rape, and murder, but it was always a local decision, made on the spot. Here was a document that urged troops to commit atrocities as part of general policy throughout the army and throughout the provinces. Bolívar did not object to the plan, since he had adopted terror as one of his tactics. However, he

The port city of Cartagena, Colombia (as it appears today), was almost completely destroyed during a siege in 1815.

did modify it somewhat. In June 1813 he proclaimed that all Europeans who did not "actively and effectively" help the "patriots" would be put to death. All "Americans" serving with the Spaniards would be pardoned for their atrocities, and all Europeans who sided with the patriots would be spared *for the time being.*[6] This last phrase was chilling, for it meant that any turncoat would be watched constantly and could be denounced for any reason. "Spaniards and Canarians [natives of the Canary Islands who served under Monteverde], be sure of death even if neutral unless you act effectively for American liberty! Americans, be sure of life even if guilty!"[7]

The War to the Death violated even the loosest rules of war and the laws of European nations. It succeeded, however, in its purpose. Every royalist in Venezuela suddenly was in danger of losing his life or of being imprisoned or persecuted. Venezuelan soldiers serving with Monteverde began deserting or joining Bolívar. Officers, who could see that they were losing on all fronts, began to look out for their own safety rather than digging in to defend Caracas. As Bolívar advanced into Venezuela, he ordered or permitted the execution of prisoners and anyone suspected of aiding the Spanish cause.

Although Bolívar never had more than seventeen hundred troops under his command, he gave false reports of their numbers and spread rumors of his overwhelming strength. The enemy fled before him, and he easily entered Caracas on August 6, 1813, at the head of only eight hundred troops. He received a hero's welcome. Twelve young women dressed in white greeted him and crowned him with a laurel wreath and presented him with flowers. Dressed in full uniform, he stood in the plaza and accepted the cheers and the applause of the crowds. The city authorities gave him the official title of "El Libertador," The Liberator, which he preferred over all other titles he was to attain in the future.[8]

Bolívar's triumph was a great one, but the battle was far from over. Monteverde fled to Puerto Cabello, where he awaited reinforcements from Spain. Bolívar's rival Mariño controlled the eastern third of the country, and there was an army in the south composed of fierce llaneros sympathetic to the Spanish. Bolívar now more than ever needed a unified and loyal armed force. But the jealous officers he had insulted or dismissed in New Granada complained of his methods and refused to join him. Bolívar was offered the presidency of Venezuela, but he turned it down because he could not wage war and govern the country at the same time. He accepted the role of dictator, however, which gave him unlimited control over the army and the government. He tried to reestablish order and to provide a constitution for the new republic. His real concern, however, was how strong his army was and the prevention of his enemies from overtaking his position.

Monteverde was soon reinforced with twelve hundred troops from Spain, but Bolívar's forces were able to keep them from advancing. Monteverde himself was wounded in one battle and was forced to leave the battle-field. While the threat from the north was serious, a much more dangerous situation was taking place in the south. There a Spanish renegade by the name of José Tomás Boves had organized a squadron of eight hundred crack horsemen from the vast llanos, or plains, of southern Venezuela. These llaneros were descendants of Indians, runaway slaves, and the earliest settlers of the area. Like the Indians of the North American plains, they practically lived on horseback.[9]

Earlier, in 1812, Boves had been imprisoned by an officer of the first Venezuelan republic for refusing to give up his horse trading business and join the army. He was thrown into prison where he was beaten and nearly killed. Soldiers broke into his store and murdered his trusted Indian employee and seized all his property. Even though Boves was spared, he was left with a passionate hatred of the former rebels who now ran the country. He offered his services to Monteverde, who asked him to form a squadron of cavalry. Boves recruited his men from the plains by offering them complete freedom to fight, kill, rape, and loot throughout the southern territories. All he asked for himself was that they deliver as many republican prisoners to him so that he could torture them to death—especially Creoles. Although he himself was white, his aim was to rid the plains of all white men but himself. Monteverde did not use Boves effectively during his campaigns against Bolívar, perhaps because he feared that Boves might prove stronger than he was.[10]

In February 1814, Bolívar issued his *Manifesto to the nations of the world on the War to the Death*. In this document he tried to justify his executions and murders as the only way he could prevent Spanish plots to overthrow his dictatorship. Bolivar had the power to appoint the governors of the cities and provinces under his control. He appointed and approved the actions of men who turned out to be as corrupt as any Spanish official and as bloodthirsty for revenge as Boves himself. The slaughter in the town of La Guaira, ordered by Bolívar's governor, was so horrible that observers were sickened. Small children were observed playing "on the blood and the muddy remains."[11]

Because of the results of the War to the Death, Bolívar soon lost what popularity and loyalty he had gained. His hold over the army, however, remained strong, and he achieved some notable victories. Nevertheless, Boves was advancing from the south, and the reinforced Spanish Army was moving in from the east. The Granadino officers still refused to serve under a man whom they considered an arrogant

Venezuelan, and Mariño in the east refused to come to Bolívar's aid. Bolívar realized the situation was impossible. He abandoned Caracas and led his army and civilian refugees east to join up with Mariño, who at least was on his side. He also took with him all the silver treasures from the cathedrals. The city lay stripped, empty except for some monks and nuns and those who were too old or sick to make the move to the east.[12]

Even the combined forces of Bolívar and Mariño were unable to halt Boves's advance, however. At the battle of La Puerta in June 1814, Boves won a decisive victory over the republican forces, and from then on he was unstoppable. People feared him so much that whole cities surrendered just on the rumor that he was nearby. He entered Caracas in July and practically wiped out everyone who was left in that city. The commander of the Spanish forces complained to his superiors in Madrid that Boves was ruining the country. Madrid, rather than stopping him, thanked Boves for his services to Spain. Boves was finally brought down when he was killed at the bloody battle of Urica in December 1814, just as he was defeating Bolívar's old friend General José Felix Ribas. Still, he had crushed the new republic, which had lasted only eleven months.

Bolívar returned to New Granada, where he was hailed as a hero. He still had the support of the Venezuelan troops, and he was appointed Commander in Chief of the army. This was done over the protests of Granadino Army officers who had been dismissed or ignored once Bolívar had been victorious in Venezuela. Now they accused him of having abandoned his troops in Venezuela and of wanting to become dictator of New Granada. Realizing that he would never gain enough support in New Granada to realize his ambitions, Bolívar again went into exile—to the island of Jamaica, which was then a British colony.

THE FINAL
RETURN

In Europe, Napoleon had been defeated in 1814 and Ferdinand VII returned to Spain. Ferdinand turned out to be a poor king. He was determined to restore an absolute monarchy, with himself as its head. He repealed the new constitution and persecuted the liberals. On the same day that Bolívar set sail for Jamaica, Ferdinand announced his desire to regain control of Spain's American colonies. All the years of struggle, bloodshed, and sacrifice by the South American rebels were to be for nothing.

Ferdinand sent his best general, Don Pablo Morillo, to Venezuela with an army of more than ten thousand troops. Morillo's orders were to put down any resistance to Spanish authority and to punish those who had led the war for independence. On April 7, 1815, Morillo landed on Margarita Island, off the coast of Venezuela, and quickly captured it and the nearby cities on the mainland. His orders were to treat the "patriots" fairly and not to allow his men to loot or murder. The remaining military leader of the South American rebels on the island was Juan Bautista Arizmendi, a cruel and ruthless man, constantly plotting against his fellow generals, including Bolívar. Morillo granted a pardon to the defeated Arizmendi in exchange for his oath of loyalty. Morillo then turned to the reconquest of South America.

In Jamaica, Bolívar had hoped to receive some backing from the British for his continued struggle against Spain. He hoped to convince them that an independent Spanish America would provide enormous opportunities for England in the form of trade and commerce. He even proposed that certain portions of Panama and Nicaragua could be turned over to England for commercial development. However, England did not wish to offend Spain, its former ally against Napoleon, by backing its most relentless enemy.

Bolívar was now no longer rich since he had lost all his land and had spent or bargained away all of the silver he had taken out of Caracas. He no longer had a real base of power, and he spent most of his time writing pamphlets and letters repeating his objectives and the good that could from them if they were achieved.

In September 1815, Bolívar wrote his famous La Carta de Jamaica, The Letter from Jamaica, in which he summarized in more detail the difficulties that Spanish America was having in its struggle for independence. The chief of these was lack of unity. He also expressed his doubts about the possibility of a democracy, like that of the United States, in Spanish America. "As long as our fellow citizens do not acquire the talents and virtues that distinguish our brothers to the north," he wrote, "a radical democratic system, far from being good for us, will bring ruin upon us. Unfortunately we do not possess those traits." He favored a strong, central government under the direction of one man to bind "the wounds and scars made by despotism and war." And throughout he expressed confidence in final victory: "A people that loves freedom will in the end be free."[1]

Bolívar's lack of money also put a crimp in his style, for he loved to attend and give parties and dance until dawn. His socializing may even have saved his life. One night he was away from home, spending the evening with a young woman he had met. His servant, not knowing that Bolívar was gone and that someone else was sleeping in his hammock, stabbed the sleeping figure. It was charged that the servant was bribed by agents of Morillo to commit the deed, but there is some evidence that the bribe had come from officials in Cartagena. Bolívar let it be known far and wide that an assassination attempt had been made on him by the official agent of the Spanish crown, Morillo.[2]

By September 1815, Morillo had reconquered almost all of Venezuela and had laid siege to Cartagena in New Granada. By November the situation was critical for the defenders of Cartagena, and a group of prominent Cartagena citizens sent a delegation to Jamaica to invite Bolívar to return and take command of the city. The offer had been made before, but Bolívar had turned it down because he had no army to back him. But this time he was offered the use of two ships, a large supply of guns, and as many men as could be crowded onto the ships. Bolívar realized that he was getting nowhere with the British in Jamaica, and he accepted the offer. He left Jamaica on December 18, 1815, but on the way he found out that the city had fallen to Morillo. The ships changed course and sailed to the island of Haiti, which was known to be friendly to refugees from the wars to the south.

Haiti was an all-black republic, the product of the only successful slave rebellion in history. It was also the only free country in the Western Hemisphere except for the United States. Its president, Alexandre Pétion, welcomed Bolívar and granted him a safe place where he could prepare himself for another expedition to

Venezuela. Bolívar openly asked Pétion for support in his mission. He promised that when he was successful, he would abolish slavery completely in all the lands he won back from Spain. Both sides in the struggles for independence had sought to gain support from their black inhabitants, but none had gone so far as Bolívar in his pledge to Pétion. Pétion agreed to provide Bolívar with whatever he needed.

Bolívar now had the backing of the government of Haiti and the support of the Granadinos, who had convinced him to come out of exile. He felt confident enough to make it plain to everyone who the leader of the expedition would be. There were many prominent men from Venezuela and New Grenada who had also come to Haiti, and Bolívar now called them together. They appointed him Commander in Chief of the expedition. With their backing, he was ready to go ahead with his plans.

The expedition sailed from Haiti on April 10, 1816, and arrived off Margarita Island on May 2. After a brief naval battle, Bolívar's force landed on the island. Margarita was already in friendly hands because the island had revolted soon after Morillo had moved on to Caracas and Cartagena. Bolívar next moved his forces to the mainland opposite Margarita, where he found most of the towns and villages practically deserted. It appeared that the inhabitants were not eager to be freed and had fled rather than become involved in a battle. Two of Bolívar's officers, his former rival Mariño and Mariño's second in command, Manuel Piar, asked for supplies and men so that they could advance inland and recruit for the army. These two, although they had sworn loyalty to Bolívar, intended to form their own armies and strike out on their own. Bolívar let them go, and they never returned. The expedition had begun badly and soon got worse.

After several skirmishes with Spanish troops, Bolívar actually abandoned his army and sailed up the coast to safety. When it began to look as though his fellow officers would openly revolt against him, Bolívar decided to return to his ships. For the third time, he left his country still in the hands of his enemies.

Bolívar returned to Haiti, where he was met by Pétion. "You have failed," he wrote to Bolívar; "such things happen; you will succeed."[3] Pétion's reaction was not unusual. Practically everyone in a high position who knew Bolívar expressed confidence in his abilities. Even his sworn enemies admitted that he was the only one among them who seemed able to unite, even partially, the different elements in Spanish American politics and society. Among his fellow military leaders—Mariño, Piar, Arizmendi—Bolívar was the only one who had a vision, which he never tired of explaining in letters, pamphlets, and speeches. It was a vision of a united South America, a republic similar to the United States of America. It was not long before even his harshest opponents in Venezuela and New Granada were appealing to him to return to carry on the fight against Morillo.

Cartagena had fallen to Morillo on June 12, 1815, after a siege of 116 days. The military and government officials of the city had fled, taking with them all the valuables they could gather. Morillo insisted that his officers and troops treat the starving people kindly. He even arranged for badly needed food supplies to be delivered to the city. He next moved on to Bogotá, the other principal city of New Granada, which he occupied easily. It was while he was on his way to take up residence in Bogotá that he learned of the revolt on Margarita island. Arizmendi had broken his vow of loyalty to Morillo and had raised an army to retake the island. He had attacked two garrisons of Spanish troops without warning and put to death all of the defenders. When Morillo heard this, he changed his attitude toward his defeated enemies. He abandoned his policy of forgiveness and began to order the executions that had become a mark of the entire struggle between Spain and her colonies.

In Haiti, Bolívar was once again persuaded to return to Venezuela to take up the war against Morillo. This time, however, he was not granted all the powers he had previously requested. He was told by the prominent Venezuelan citizens and fellow military leaders that he should take care of military matters only and not bother with the administration of the government. He was also told that he would not be dictator. Bolívar agreed to these conditions and sailed for Venezuela on December 21, 1816. When Morillo heard this, he decided to lead his army back to Venezuela and personally take charge of the war in the east.[4]

At this time, Bolívar had three rivals in the patriot forces. There was Mariño, who thought of himself as "El Libertador" of the west and commanded an army of two thousand men. Mariño's former second in command, Piar, a man of mixed race, had the loyalty of most nonwhite soldiers among the patriots. He was a fine soldier who controlled the eastern province of Guyana, but he obeyed no orders but his own and was known for his execution of prisoners. Then there was José Antonio Páez, another plainsman who had succeeded Boves as leader of the llaneros. Although Boves had fought for Spain and Páez was on the side of the South American rebels, it made no difference to the llaneros. They fought for a leader who could promise them victory and the destruction and looting that went with it, and it didn't make much difference which side he was on.

At first, Bolívar did not try to unite these three fiercely independent men. He took his own small force of men and tried to retake Caracas and reclaim his property. He was defeated decisively and had to retreat to the east and the protection of the armies of Mariño

General José Antonio Páez, leader of the hard-riding
Venezuelan plainsmen, holds a lance which was the main
weapon of his cavalrymen.

and Piar. Bolívar now decided that he would have to consolidate the three forces against Morillo. He began with Páez and won him over with the offer of the rank of brigadier general if he would recognize Bolívar as head of the army. Páez accepted the offer, perhaps because he wanted recognition by any future government that Bolívar might form. Mariño was more difficult. Since he considered himself as much "El Libertador" as Bolívar, he called a congress and attempted to form a government. This attempt failed through lack of support from Bolívar and the officials who backed him. Mariño was ordered to report to Guyana, a province to the east of Venezuela, which was then under Bolívar's control.

Morillo was attacking in the north, trying to regain Margarita island and punish Arizmendi. He despised Arizmendi for breaking his vow of loyalty and resuming the war. Bolívar concentrated his activities inland on the Orinoco River. He tried to get Piar to join him there, but the young officer had won some stunning victories over the Spanish forces and refused to put himself under Bolívar's control. When Piar announced that he was going off on his own, Bolívar had him arrested and charged with desertion. The court-martial, which was completely controlled by Bolívar, found Piar guilty and sentenced him to death. Bolívar was now in charge, and he had a strong base on the Orinoco River from which he could be resupplied by sea. He set up his headquarters in Angostura (now Bolívar City), on the Orinoco River, and began to establish a government that would be recognized by the rest of the world.

In late February 1819, Bolívar called the Congress of Angostura at which he presented his ideas for a new republic and a new constitution. Although the new constitution was modeled after that of the United States, it did not call for the same degree of democracy. After all, most of the people allowed to vote in Venezuela were in the military, and they were under control of their superiors. It did call for sensible taxation, distribution of wealth, and representative government. However, it also called for a hereditary senate like the English House of Lords, and a president who was elected for life. This was more like a constitutional monarchy, such as England's, than a republic. Bolívar also recommended the complete abolition of slavery, finally making good on his promise to the president of Haiti. The congress voted in favor of freeing the slaves, but nothing ever came of the resolution. (Slavery was not officially abolished in Venezuela until 1854.) Bolívar then resigned as chief commander and left to allow the congress to vote on his recommendations. The congress turned down his resignation and elected him president for life. Bolívar accepted, and then turned the government over to his chosen vice-president and went back to waging war.

Fortunately for Bolívar and others waging wars of independence, the end of the Napoleonic Wars had left a large number of unemployed officers and experienced soldiers in England. Many of these chose to sign on as mercenaries for foreign countries, the most convenient of which were the newly independent states of Spanish America. Bolívar's backers had sent agents to London to enlist as many of these mercenaries as possible, and now a stream of them began to arrive in Venezuela. The South American rebel army had been highly unstable, with men deserting before or after every battle, and its makeup consisted of warring races and classes. The mercenaries gave Bolívar the closest thing to a solid core of dependable troops. He used them with success in battle after battle.

Bolívar's other source of dependable troops were the bands of llaneros from the south, but they were sworn to follow their leader Páez and nobody else. Páez was firmly in control of the vast plains bordering on the Apure River and saw no reason to fight to regain some distant province. Bolívar pleaded personally for Páez to join him in a campaign against New Granada to regain Venezuela for the republican forces. Páez was skeptical, but when he saw what an excellent horseman Bolívar was, he decided that here was someone who could be a worthy companion in battle. Páez and his cavalry prized horsemanship over everything else. Bolívar won over one of his most important allies not with statesmanship, eloquence, or charm, but by his ability to handle a horse.

Morillo was still trying to capture the northern ports and Margarita Island for Spain. He was doing this mainly to punish the "hypocritical and despicable" Arizmendi,[5] who was heading the defense of the island. Morillo had drawn off most of his troops from New Granada. General Santander was now in command of the South American Granadino Army, but he was barely holding his own. Bolívar believed that if he could join up with Santander, they could push the remaining Spanish forces out of New Granada. Thus began his epic march over the plains and through the swamps and jungles of Venezuela, up the steep approaches to the Andes and finally over the mountains themselves to the high plains of Colombia.

THE REPUBLIC OF GRAN COLOMBIA

 After his victory at Boyacá and his triumphant entry into Bogotá in 1819, Bolívar turned to the governing of his new possession. He renamed it Gran Colombia, the new Republic of Greater Colombia, and saw it as part of one unified country with Venezuela. He appointed the twenty-seven-year-old Santander as his vice-president to run the provisional government, and then left for Venezuela to resume the war with Morillo.

When Bolívar arrived back in Angostura, he quickly called his congress and offered them a new constitution for the Republic of Gran Colombia. A vice-president would be appointed for each of the three provinces—Colombia (formerly New Granada), Venezuela, and Ecuador (which had yet to be liberated). Bolívar would be over-all president. His reason for doing this was to convince the rest of the world that the wars for independence were being conducted by a unified nation under a strong leader and a central government. He sent agents to London and the United States to present this new, revised picture of the Republic of Gran Colombia and to try to secure loans and material support.

The war against Morillo was not going well, however. Caracas and Cartagena were still in Spanish hands, and Morillo was expecting reinforcements from Spain. Bolívar visited Páez on the Apure River on January 10, 1820, in the hope of getting him to join in a direct attack on Morillo. Páez refused, on the grounds that his cavalry was too weak as a result of an epidemic among his horses. Bolívar, whose own forces were reduced due to desertions, decided to continue on to Colombia and join up with Santander's remaining army. From there he directed several campaigns throughout the two provinces, but nothing seemed to go right. He was having trouble with his own ambitious and headstrong officers. "Wherever I go," he wrote in a letter, "there is disunity and disorder."[1]

The situation turned around suddenly when it was learned that in January 1820 a series of uprisings in Spain had put an end to Ferdinand VII's hopes for crushing the independence movements in South America. Ferdinand was forced to reestablish the cortes, the Spanish parliament or congress, and to accept a constitution that severely limited his powers. In May a delegation sent by the governor of Caracas informed Morillo of the situation in Spain. Its members asked that Venezuela also adopt the new constitution of Spain and make peace with the South American rebel forces. Morillo, who had been weakened by a wound, was discouraged by his failure to bring about a final victory over the rebels and was only too glad to follow orders. He declared a month-long armistice in which his army would stop fighting if the rebels would do the same.

Bolívar welcomed this armistice, not because it might lead to peace, but because it gave him a chance to regroup and strengthen his forces for a new campaign against Morillo. He tried to retake Cartagena before the armistice went into effect, but failed. He asked Páez to mount an offensive and capture the strategic town of Barinas, but Páez replied that he could not because the plains were flooded. Bolívar finally agreed to the armistice with Morillo, and the two men met in the village of Santa Ana on November 27, 1820. Morillo arrived at the meeting in full dress uniform with his staff of officers and a number of mounted troops. Bolívar arrived with only twelve officers dressed in their battle uniforms.

The next day friendly negotiations began, and a six-month truce was signed. Morillo was convinced that his campaign could never be won without massive reinforcements, which Ferdinand VII could not supply without permission from the cortes. Besides, Morillo was eager to return home, which he did on December 16, 1820. He left in command General Miguel de la Torre, a much less capable and decisive leader who, in addition, was married to a relative of Bolívar. "This in itself," Bolívar later admitted, "was an immense victory."[2]

The armistice had given Bolívar the time to rebuild his forces and improve his position by maneuvering his forces in violation of the truce. One of the provisions of the armistice agreement was that the opposing forces could visit relatives and friends in territory occupied by the enemy. This was fine for the native Venezuelans and Granadinos who fought on both sides, but the Spanish soldiers had nowhere to go. This was all in keeping with Bolívar's aim to win back the affection and the confidence of the people. Many Venezuelans who had fought for the Spanish decided to stay with their rebel countrymen. Bolívar's agents abroad were also making headway in gaining acceptance of Gran Colombia as a legitimate nation. In the United States, Henry Clay, a statesman, had made a motion in the Senate to recognize the independence of the governments of

South America. The motion did not pass, but it at least opened the door to future acceptance.[3]

Bolívar resumed the war. Caracas was under siege by the rebels, and the defending forces of La Torre were virtually surrounded. On June 24, 1821, Bolívar began a three-pronged attack from the west, east, and south and forced the enemy into an open battle at Carabobo, just south of Puerto Cabello. Though Páez nearly lost the battle through his rashness and inexperience, the British mercenaries held fast until Bolívar could attack with his main force. La Torre lost control of his troops, who feared reprisals from the patriots and either fled the field or joined the rebels.

Monument to the Battle of Carabobo, which was fought on June 24, 1821. It was Bolivar's last major victory in Venezuela.

Bolívar entered Caracas on June 29, 1821, but did not receive the reception he expected. Most of the people had run away, fearing the usual looting and executions that inevitably followed a triumph by either side in the war. Bolívar tried to ease these fears by treating the few people who remained to a series of entertainments that lasted for days. Bolívar offered generous surrender terms to the remaining Spanish forces, and they soon gave in. In November, Cartagena in the west finally surrendered, and Bolívar was in almost complete control of the two provinces of Venezuela and Colombia.

Bolívar moved quickly to reorganize Venezuela as part of Gran Colombia. Although it had the name of a republic, it was governed along military lines. Bolívar appointed a trustworthy friend as vice-president of the province, but he appointed Páez as military and civil commander. He knew the risks in putting the young and headstrong cavalryman in charge, but he could not afford to antagonize him by reducing his authority. Bolívar was eager to return to action in the west and conquer one of the last remaining outposts of the Spanish empire—Ecuador, with its capital in Quito. He had already declared Ecuador as part of the Republic of Gran Colombia, and he wanted to make it a reality.

Bolívar had another very important reason for wanting to establish his presence in Ecuador. Before he had ended the armistice and marched on Caracas,

Bolívar had learned that General José de San Martín, the liberator of Argentina, had occupied Lima, Peru. The Spanish forces in the southwest were now retreating northward before the rebel forces. San Martín was Bolívar's only rival in the liberation of Spanish America. He had already freed Argentina and had helped Chile gain her independence. It was beginning to appear that he would achieve the final liberation of all of Spanish America and gain the title of the true "El Libertador."

San Martín had been born in the viceroyalty of Buenos Aires (now Argentina) in 1778, into a military family. He spent twenty years in the Spanish Army, serving throughout Europe and North Africa. In 1812 he returned to Buenos Aires where he joined in the revolutionary movement that was sweeping Spanish America. He organized and trained a revolutionary army, which took over the government of Buenos Aires. He declared the independence of the United Provinces (as Argentina was then called) on July 9, 1816. The next year he invaded Chile and took the capital city of Santiago from the Spanish. He won a decisive battle against the Spanish at Maypo on April 2, 1818. The way was now open for the invasion of Peru, the last Spanish stronghold in South America. San Martín entered Peru's capital city, Lima, on July 12, 1821. Two weeks later he proclaimed Peru's independence from Spain, but the country north of Lima was still occupied by the Spanish Army.

This statue of General San Martín is located at the Avenue of the Americas entrance to Central Park in New York City.

Throughout most of 1821, Bolívar was concerned with internal affairs in Venezuela. He had urged Santander, who was in command in the west, to begin a campaign in the south to take Ecuador, but several battles and skirmishes had proven fruitless for both sides. Bolívar put General Antonio José de Sucre in charge of an army that invaded Ecuador from the sea, at the port city of Guayaquil on the coast of the Pacific Ocean. Bolívar took charge of the army that invaded from the north. He was nearly defeated in a battle at Bomboná on April 22, 1822, but Sucre won a decisive victory at Pichincha outside of Quito. The Spanish forces finally surrendered on June 6, 1822, and Bolívar entered Quito in triumph on June 15, 1822.

In Peru, San Martín was having trouble with his officers and his troops as his campaign became stalled. His army was smaller than the Spanish forces holding the mountainous country to the north of him. His men were grumbling and deserting because of the lack of booty, and his foreign mercenaries abandoned him. To control the situation, he declared himself dictator of Peru. He decided that his only chance for success was to join forces with Bolívar, who was still enjoying his triumph in Quito and strengthening his claim to Ecuador as part of Gran Colombia. The two men met at the Pacific port city of Guayaquil and conferred briefly before attending a banquet. Bolívar offered the toast: "To the two greatest men in South America—General

Quito, in present-day Ecuador, was the scene of one of Bolívar's greatest victory parades.

San Martín and myself." San Martín, a professional soldier with no ambitions for himself, responded simply, "To the early end of the war; to the organization of the republics of the continent and to the health of the Liberator of Colombia."[4]

The next day the two men met alone for four hours. What was said or what they decided remained a mystery for many years, for neither man left any record of the meeting except for a few letters. From these and other sources, however, scholars have been able to piece together what was agreed on between them at Guayaquil. First, San Martín accepted that Ecuador was now part of Gran Colombia. Second, he offered to serve under Bolívar if he joined him in the conquest of Peru, but Bolívar refused. Bolívar offered a few troops to reinforce San Martín's army, but San Martín thought this was not enough. San Martín felt that Peru was not ready for a republican form of government on the order of Gran Colombia and thought that a royal family from Europe should govern under a constitution. Bolívar, to whom any idea of a king in America was impossible, refused outright. San Martín appears to have been dissatisfied with the meeting, for that evening he silently left a ball in his honor and set sail for Peru.[5]

San Martín was tired of the endless bickering and intrigues of both military and public life, and his health was failing. After returning to Lima, he presented his resignation to the congress that he had set up under his dictatorship. He retired to his farm in Argentina, where he lived until 1824. Then, discouraged by the continual strife among the people he had served so selflessly, he sailed for Europe, where he settled in Belgium. He died in Paris, France, in 1850, having never returned to his homeland.

With San Martín gone, Bolívar was now the undisputed leader of Spanish America. In Venezuela, groups were plotting to separate from Gran Colombia. In Colombia, the congress resented Bolívar's neglect of the government and his constant drain of the country's resources in order to finance his campaigns. In Lima the government was coming apart due to internal struggles among rivals for power. The Spanish Army still held the highlands of Upper Peru, which meant that they could hold out until the political situation changed in Spain and help could be sent.

Everyone knew that Bolívar was the only man who could unite all parties and expel the Spanish. He finally received permission from the congress in Bogotá to go to Peru. In September 1823 he sailed to Callao, the port city for the capital city of Lima. The Peruvians made him supreme dictator, and he soon found out that this made him the head of a government that was corrupt and barely able to function. There was little money for the upcoming campaign in Upper Peru, and the only officer Bolívar could trust was Sucre.

CHAPTER EIGHT

PLOWING
THE SEA

On August 5, 1824, Bolívar met the Spanish army of eleven thousand men on a plain before the Junin hills southeast of Lima. Bolívar had a force of seven thousand men. The battle was highlighted by a charge of the Spanish cavalry, which was broken up by Colombians armed only with long spears. Not a shot was fired. The struggle lasted into the night, and no one knew who had the upper hand. Bolívar, who was stricken with soroche (altitude sickness), did not take part. At one point he thought the battle was lost.[1] Word was finally brought to him that the Spanish were retreating. Bolívar put Sucre in command, ordering him to tend to the wounded, collect all his forces, and continue the campaign against the rapidly retreating enemy. Bolívar returned to Lima, where he spent his time trying to raise reinforcements for Sucre.

On December 12, 1824, Sucre met the Spanish forces at Ayacucho on a small plain at the foot of a chain of mountains. The Spanish had about seven thousand men and the allied army of Colombians and Peruvians had fifty-seven hundred. The two forces faced each other at sunrise.

The battle began. The Spanish forces had the advantage at first, but then two Spanish regiments acted against orders and ran into the fray to share in the victory. Sucre took advantage of this and threw in reinforcements who advanced on the Spanish with courage and discipline. The Spanish general Juan Antonio Monet was sent to halt the advance, but he soon gave way before the relentless charge of the allied force. Confusion and panic took hold of the Spanish forces. In two hours the allies managed to surround and defeat the last Spanish Army of any importance on the continent.

Bolívar returned to Lima. Most of the officers and men of the Spanish Army who had surrendered joined his allied army.

Within a month's time, Great Britain formally recognized Gran Colombia as a legitimate nation and

Bolívar entered Arequipa, Peru, in triumph on May 14, 1825, and was welcomed by the victors of the battle of Ayacucho.

opened the way for other nations to do the same. The United States soon followed. Bolívar could have returned to Gran Colombia where he would have been welcomed as a great hero. He chose to remain in Peru, however, to continue the war against the remaining Spanish forces in the highlands, called Upper Peru. This was a land of mountains and high plateaus that was claimed by both Argentina and Peru but was held by the Spanish.

After his victory at Ayacucho, Sucre pursued the remaining Spanish forces into Upper Peru. The people there did not consider their country part of Peru and seemed to Sucre "to want to belong to no one but [themselves]."[2] Bolívar wanted to join Upper Peru with Peru into one republic, which could then become a part of Gran Colombia. Sucre became influenced by the people of Upper Peru who wanted freedom not only from Spain but from Peru and Buenos Aires as well. Sucre authorized an assembly of Upper Peru to decide on what sort of government the region would have. Bolívar wrote Sucre reminding him, "You are under my orders . . . and can do nothing but what I order you to do" and yet "you take it upon yourself to decide a legislative operation."[3] It was the first disagreement between the two. Sucre apologized for his actions and adjourned the assembly.

In the meantime, Sucre had defeated the Spanish force at Tumula on April 2, 1825, and Bolívar left Lima for a trip through Upper Peru. There he learned that public opinion was strongly in favor of independence. He also met with a special delegation from the neighboring state of Buenos Aires that, while thanking him for his service on behalf of Spanish America, declared that Upper Peru was free to choose its own form of government. Bolívar recalled the assembly and allowed them to vote. The assembly voted for independence and honored Bolívar by naming their country after him, *Republica Bolívar*, now known as

Copocabana, Bolivia, was a stop on Bolívar's triumphant tour through the new country named after him.

The country of Bolivia was named after The Liberator and has two capital cities. Here, its administrative capital, La Paz, is pictured.

Bolivia. They also made him dictator while he was in the country and promised that statues of him would be erected in every principal city and his portrait would hang in every public building. The new Bolivia, which was rich in silver deposits, also advanced him a large loan. Sucre also received many complimentary honors, including the naming of a city after him. Bolívar helped prepare a new constitution, and he named Sucre as the head of state of the new republic.

Throughout his career, Bolívar had insisted that he wanted nothing from public life. His ambition was to return to his estates and live the peaceful life of a country gentleman and farmer. It now seemed that he was in a position to do so. Colombia had named him president for life, Peru had made him dictator, and Bolivia was his namesake.

However, there were some problems. Santander in New Granada still thought of himself as the equal of Bolívar, and Páez in Venezuela was supporting a movement for separation from New Granada. Bolívar's dream of a Federation of the Andes composed of all the Spanish-speaking countries of South America was far from a reality. Chile and Argentina were involved in their own internal disputes and showed no desire to become part of the sort of federation Bolívar had in mind. Bolívar decided to travel north to Gran Colombia to mend his fences.

In August 1826, he announced his "Bolivian" constitution in which he declared that Santander in Colombia and Páez in Venezuela were equals in governmental powers. This, in fact, lessened Santander's powers and added to Páez's, since Santander was supposed to be vice-president of all of Gran Colombia. The country became divided between Santanderists, or liberals, and Bolivarists. The Bolivarists were called serviles (servants), after the conservatives who had backed Ferdinand VII in Spain. Bolívar, however, was still the supreme commander with unlimited powers.

Against such a troubled background, Bolívar called for a Congress of Panama. His purpose was to show the stability and union of the new independent states and gain respect in Europe and the United States. These northern countries were their trading partners and their only source of money. He wanted the congress to be strictly an affair of Spanish America and did not invite the United States. Santander invited them anyway, but their representatives did not arrive on time.[4] England sent only an unofficial observer. One of the reasons Bolívar had chosen Panama was to impress England with the advantages of building a canal there to join the Atlantic and Pacific oceans. Chile could not send a delegation because the country was leaderless with no one in charge to name a delegation. Argentina's government was barely established and declined to

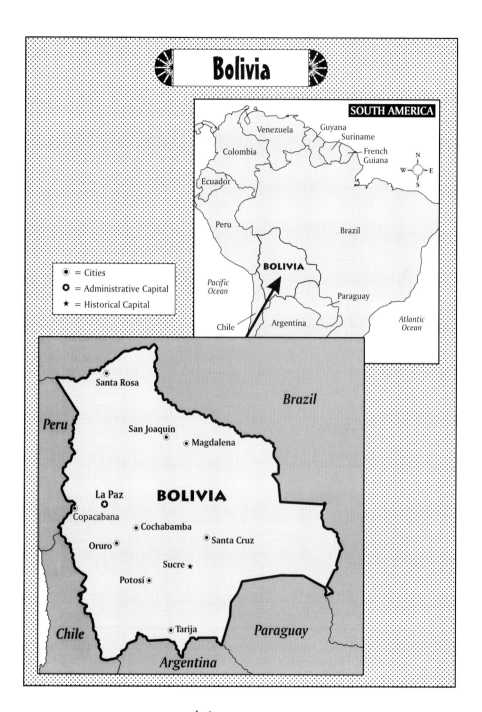

Bolivia

SOUTH AMERICA

Venezuela
Guyana
Suriname
Colombia
French
Guiana
Ecuador
N
W E
S
Peru
Brazil
BOLIVIA
Pacific
Ocean
Paraguay
Chile
Argentina
Atlantic
Ocean

◉ = Cities
✪ = Administrative Capital
★ = Historical Capital

Santa Rosa

Brazil

Peru

San Joaquin
◉ Magdalena

La Paz
✪
BOLIVIA
Copacabana
◉ Cochabamba
Oruro ◉
◉ Santa Cruz
Sucre ★
Potosí ◉

Chile
◉ Tarija
Paraguay
Argentina

Map of Bolivia

attend due to internal struggles, which were soon to topple its president.

The congress opened on June 22, 1826, and lasted a little longer than three weeks. Only Colombia, Peru, Mexico, and Guatemala attended formally, and they accomplished little. They agreed to a treaty of mutual help and defense, but none could be sure that their governments back home would approve. Bolívar was not pleased with the outcome and disagreed with some of the articles of the treaty.

The Congress of Panama was not a success. Nevertheless, it showed the world that the former colonies were serious in their intentions of forming stable governments and engaging in diplomatic activity with the society of nations. It was also the forerunner of such later organizations as the Pan-American Union in the 1890s and the Organization of American States in the twentieth century.

While the Congress of Panama tried to show unity, Bolívar's Republic of Gran Colombia was splitting apart. Páez had broken the constitution on April 30, 1826, and had seized power in Venezuela. He declared that he would no longer take orders from the government in Bogotá, where Santander ran things as Bolívar's vice-president. Bolívar decided to return to Bogotá to reestablish his authority. He was again voted full powers by the congress.

Bolívar suspected Santander of plotting against him, but confirmed him as his vice-president while he continued on to Venezuela to deal with Páez. Bolívar distrusted both men, but Páez was, above all, a soldier, while Santander had given up the military life for that of a politician and lawyer. Páez also had his llaneros who were devoted to him, while Santander had to rely on unpopular methods such as drafting troops. Bolívar chose to back the soldier rather than the lawyer, and by so doing approved of the split between Venezuela and Colombia. When he met with Páez, he pardoned him for his actions and reconfirmed him as the chief military and civil authority in Venezuela. Santander began actively to plot against Bolívar by spreading rumors and publishing anonymous articles critical of Bolívar in all the newspapers of Colombia.

Further troubles were rising in Peru, where ambitious army officers were trying to gain power from Bolívar's representatives. Santander encouraged them, just as he would encourage any movement or party that opposed Bolívar. In the new country of Bolivia, envious and ambitious rivals were showing opposition to Sucre, and even Ecuador was beginning to object to Bolívar's absolute powers and what his enemies called his high-handed methods. Whenever Bolívar was actually present in a country or city, the people and their leaders never failed to welcome him with open arms. They would often grant him even more powers than he had held at the time of their liberation. But as soon as he left, the local leaders would begin to argue among themselves and try to take back the powers they had given to Bolívar. The loss of central governmental control was spreading throughout the five countries. Bolívar's Gran Republic was crumbling.

Secret groups began forming in opposition to Bolívar, who was being called a tyrant and a despot in journals and pamphlets that men such as Santander financed and distributed. Bolívar was even accused of wanting to be the emperor of Spanish America.

When Bolívar returned to Bogotá from Venezuela in June 1828, he was not met with the usual outpouring of love and support. In August he issued a decree intended to get rid of Santander by abolishing the office of vice-president and setting up a council of state with himself as *Libertador-Presidente*. He now had more power, which he had granted to himself, than any Spanish viceroy had ever possessed. Furthermore, he had direct control over the life and welfare of every one of the citizens of his "republic."

One secret group was led by a young Frenchman, Augustin Horment, and a Venezuelan Army officer named Pedro Carujo. Its plan was to assassinate Bolívar on August 10, 1828, during a masked ball to celebrate the Battle of Boyacá. However, Bolívar, who usually could not resist the chance to dance the night away, left early. Santander had been conveniently out of town, and when he returned he met with the conspirators. They now planned to murder Bolívar on September 20. Santander refused to go along with the plot, at least while he was in the country. The plot was put off until October, but events suddenly got out of hand.

On September 25, 1828, Captain Benedicto Triana entered the artillery barracks in Bogotá and drunkenly announced that he was going to "do in that old man Bolívar"[5] and that he had the support of powerful friends. The officer in charge reported the incident to the commander of the Bogotá garrison, Colonel Ramón Guerra. Guerra told him to lock up the man. Guerra himself, however, was one of the plotters against Bolívar, and he quickly warned his fellow conspirators that something had gone wrong. Several men were sent to the artillery barracks to arm and get ready, but most lost their nerve. At midnight, Horment with ten civilians and Carujo with sixteen soldiers entered the palace where Bolívar was sleeping. Horment and his civilians killed three sentries and then broke down the door to Bolívar's quarters and subdued a lieutenant who was on duty.

Bolívar was sleeping in the next room. Watching over him was his companion of several years, Manuela Sáenz. She had been one of the maidens dressed in white who had greeted Bolívar on his triumphal entry into Quito in 1822. Since then she had accompanied him everywhere. She had always had great influence over Bolívar, for which she was despised by his advisers as well as by his enemies. Bolívar had asked her to keep him company, because he feared that a revolution was coming.

Around midnight Manuela heard dogs bark, followed by some strange noises. She woke Bolívar, who leaped out of bed and grabbed his pistol and sword. He rushed to open the door, but Manuela held him back and told him to get dressed. He put on his clothes and said, "Bravo, now I am dressed. What do we do? Barricade ourselves?" Manuela rushed to the window, opened it, and motioned Bolívar to come over. "You are right," he said and went to the window. She looked out and when she saw the way was clear, motioned for him to go. Bolívar leaped out of the window just as the door was being forced open. The conspirators entered to find only a woman with sword in hand staring at them defiantly.[6]

Bolívar escaped by hiding under a bridge for three hours while horsemen galloped by and shots were fired. He finally made his way to the main square where he was greeted with joy by his loyal officers and men. "Do you want to kill me with joy when I am on the point of dying with grief?" he said.[7] Order was soon established and the conspirators rounded up. Manuela had been severely beaten but had survived. Fourteen of the conspirators, including Horment, were executed. Carujo was offered his life in exchange for information on the conspiracy. Santander, the man who appeared to be behind the whole thing, was reluctantly spared by Bolívar. He did this only because he knew that Santander would be made into a martyr and, therefore, would be more dangerous to him dead than alive. Instead, Bolívar banished his old adversary to Cartagena to wait for a ship to take him into exile in France.

The attempt on his life was the saddest blow Bolívar had ever experienced in what had seemed a charmed life. Since his days in Peru he had been ill and was now exhausted. Bolívar called his ministers and advisers together and announced that he was going to call the national assembly into session and surrender all his powers. Once again, he said that he wanted to retire. His proposal was rejected. Everyone attending the meeting knew that without Bolívar the whole government of Gran Colombia would collapse.

Bolívar's friends and advisers began to talk of a constitutional monarchy as the solution to Gran Colombia's problems. Bolívar, of course, would be named king, but would be controlled by a congress, or parliament. Upon his death or resignation, a European prince would be named as his successor, since Bolívar had no children. Bolívar rejected the idea, causing more dissatisfaction among his advisers and friends.

In the south, Peru's revolt had turned serious when the Peruvian Navy blockaded Colombia's Pacific Ocean ports and assembled an army ready to invade Ecuador. Bolívar put Sucre in charge of the army and prepared to go south to take part in the campaign. He was so weak that he could not ride more than a few miles at a time. Sucre defeated the Peruvian Army at Tarqui and offered the Peruvians generous terms of surrender. This irritated Bolívar, who wanted to punish Peru. Sucre felt that war with Peru was unnecessary, so Bolívar turned to his other officers. He launched a needless and disastrous campaign during the rainy season against the port city of Guayaquil. After suffering many losses because of disease and exposure, the exhausted army arrived at Guayaquil only to find that the city had already surrendered. Bolívar was now seriously ill, and his officers began to question his ability to lead an army, much less a nation. One of his leading generals, José María Córdova, revolted and declared that he would "conquer power [that is, Bolívar] in order to put it under the safeguard of law."[8] His small army of followers was defeated by Bolívar's troops, and he died from his wounds.

Bolívar's troubles with Peru and with Córdova's revolt gave Páez in Venezuela the opportunity he had been waiting for. He charged that Bolívar was responsible for all of Venezuela's woes and called him a tyrant. He declared Venezuela completely independent

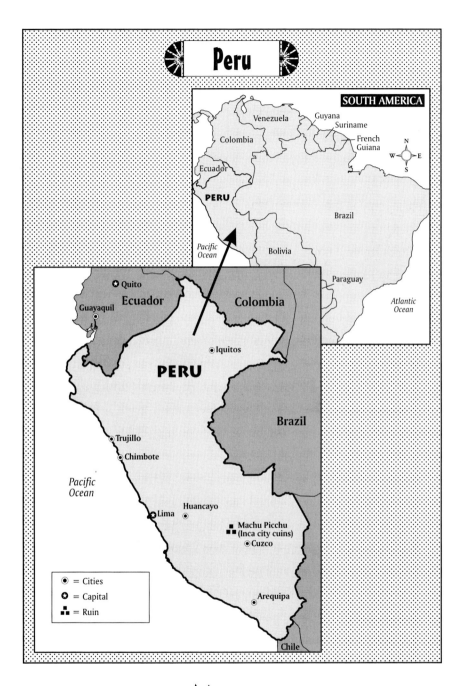

Peru

SOUTH AMERICA

Venezuela
Guyana
Suriname
Colombia
French
Guiana
Ecuador
N
W · E
S
PERU
Brazil
Pacific
Ocean
Bolivia
Paraguay
Atlantic
Ocean

☉ Quito
Ecuador
Colombia
Guayaquil
☉ Iquitos
PERU
Brazil
☉ Trujillo
☉ Chimbote
Pacific
Ocean
Huancayo
☉ Lima   ☉
■ Machu Picchu
■ ■ (Inca city cuins)
☉ Cuzco
☉ = Cities
☉ = Capital
▪▪ = Ruin
☉ Arequipa
Chile

Map of Peru

of Gran Colombia, and the congress backed him by rejecting Bolívar's authority. Páez was given complete military and civil power in Bolívar's native land and the source of all his wealth and glory.

Bolívar returned to Bogotá in January 1830, and his friends and advisers were shocked at his appearance. His disease, which was probably tuberculosis, had made him pale and weak. He was convinced by his advisers to call another congress to determine what to do to put the government back on course. Bolívar asked Sucre to act as president of the congress. Bolívar withdrew after stating that he had faith in the congress under the leadership of Sucre, "the worthiest of all Colombian generals." By saying this he managed to offend another of his best generals, Rafael Urdaneta. Bolívar later said that it had been a slip of the tongue, that he intended to say "one of the worthiest," but the damage had been done.[9] Once again, Bolívar had lost the loyalty of one of his officers who had influence with the rest of his army.

In March, Bolívar proposed an invasion of Venezuela to regain his country from Páez. Urdaneta, the most influential of his remaining generals, said that the independence of Venezuela was a fact that everyone recognized. A war would be unpopular and useless. Bolívar's other officers agreed, and he realized that he could no longer count on his closest advisers and friends. Bolívar went ahead and attempted to organize an army for the invasion, but many of his troops mutinied and went over to the side of Páez. The congress tried to negotiate with Páez to rejoin Gran Colombia on generous terms, but Páez felt strong enough to turn down all offers that were made. Gran Colombia was no more.

Bolívar, exhausted and weakened, once again resigned and asked the congress to name his successor. They said that they could not do so until they had a new constitution and had elected leaders. Bolívar named an acting president and retired to a farm outside the city. But he had still not given up completely, and he expected to be called back to be president of Colombia. His advisers, friends, and officers, however, asked him not to put his name up for consideration by the congress. Urdaneta even advised him to leave the country.

In May 1830 the congress elected a diplomat, Joaquin Mosquera, president and canceled the remaining powers that Bolívar had been granted in the last session. Bolívar announced that he was leaving the country. When news of this reached the Venezuelan soldiers in his army, they mutinied and marched home to Venezuela. They would not serve in Colombia without Bolívar. The departure of the loyal Venezuelan soldiers now left Bolívar with little or no protection, and his few remaining backers feared an attack by the Santanderists. On his last night in Bogotá,

May 7, 1830, his friends suspected an assassination attempt and kept him company throughout the night. The next morning they rode with him on the first stage of his journey to the coast. They traveled slowly, not only because Bolívar was ill, but also because he wanted to be kept in daily contact by couriers with Bogotá. He still expected to be called back to assume his former powers and bring his creation, Gran Colombia, back together again.

His journey followed the course of the Magdalena River, the scene of his earliest triumphs. He was barely a week into his journey when he learned that Ecuador had seceded from Gran Colombia. Only a few more weeks after that, he learned that his loyal friend General Sucre had been ambushed and assassinated on June 4. Bolívar wrote bitterly: "It is impossible to live in a country where the most famous generals are cruelly and barbarously murdered, the very men to whom America owes its freedom. . . . I believe the purpose of the crime was to deprive the fatherland of my successor. I can no longer live in such a country."[10] Still, he eagerly awaited news from Bogotá that Mosquera had been forced from power and that the congress wanted him back.

Mosquera, however, showed himself to be more friendly with the Santanderists than to Bolívar, since he had allowed the conspirators in the assassination attempt of September 25 to return to Bogotá. After a series of clashes between the few Colombian troops loyal to Bolívar and those who opposed him, the government was finally forced to resign. Urdaneta, who was now in charge, invited Bolívar back to take over the presidency. By this time, Bolívar was too sick and disillusioned, and for the first time his refusal to assume power was sincere. "I have no hope of saving the fatherland,"[11] he said from his sickbed in a house near the town of Santa Marta.

Bolívar's condition worsened and he passed in and out of consciousness, sometimes talking in his delirium. On November 9, 1830, in one of his last letters, he wrote to the leader of the rebels in Ecuador to sum up what he had learned after having held power for twenty years. Some believe that what he had to say was the product of a delirious mind.[12] Others say that it was a bitter reaction to the breaking up of Gran Colombia and to the civil wars that had broken out after his loss of the presidency. He wrote:

> . . . I have derived only a few sure conclusions: first, America is ungovernable for us; second, he who serves a revolution ploughs the sea; third, the only thing that can be done in America is to emigrate; fourth, this country will fall without fail into the hands of an unbridled multitude, to pass later to petty . . . tyrants of all colors and races . . .

There was more in the same tone of despair, and he concluded with: ". . . what unfortunate peoples, what unfortunate governments!"[13]

On December 10, Bolívar was visited by the bishop of Santa Marta. After viewing Bolívar's condition and speaking with his physician, the bishop advised Bolívar to put his affairs in order. Bolívar immediately made his will and arranged to have some papers unfavorable to his colleagues burned. A week later, on December 17, 1830, he died. His last words were said to be: "Let us go, the people do not want us in this land . . . my baggage, take it on board the frigate,"[14] referring to the ship he believed was waiting in the harbor to take him into his last exile. He was forty-seven years old.

Bolívar's gloomy outlook at the end of his life seemed justified by later events. Gran Colombia was no more. Santander returned from exile and was elected president of Colombia. Ecuador was a dictatorship, and Venezuela was controlled by Páez.

Bolívar's enemies did nothing to keep his memory alive, and his body lay in a simple grave in Santa Marta. Santander died in 1840, and in 1842 Bolívar's remaining admirers convinced the government to honor their hero. His remains were brought to Caracas where he was laid to rest with great ceremony. Later in the century he was entombed in Venezuela's new national pantheon, where he lies surrounded by the nation's heroes. His birthday is now a national holiday, and statues and busts of him exist in town squares throughout South America.

Bolívar was convinced he had died a failure, but history has deemed him a success. Without him, Spanish America's liberation from Spain might have taken decades longer to accomplish. His dream of unification never became a reality, but it did give a collective identity to the peoples of Spanish America. The present makeup of the nations of northern South America was largely his doing and has remained stable, regardless of the political upheavals that have taken place there. He made the first positive step to abolish slavery in South America. In this respect, he was many years ahead of his counterparts in the United States.

Many historians and scholars find fault with Bolívar for his poor generalship, his failure to hold to treaties and agreements, his poor judgment in appointees and advisers, and above all, his ruthless executions and pursuit of the War to the Death. But none of them belittle his achievements or deny his vision. In the popular mind, he exists as one of the greatest Spanish Americans who ever lived.

103

CHRONOLOGY

1783 —Born Simón José Antonio de la Santissima Trinidad de Bolívar y Palacios, in Caracas, Venezuela, on July 24.

1799 —Goes to Spain to study.

1802—Marries María Teresa de Toro, in Madrid, Spain, on May 26. Returns with wife to Caracas in June.

1803—María Teresa dies in January. Returns to Europe. Sees Napoleon crowned emperor of France on December 2.

1805—Makes vow on Aventine Hill in Rome to work for independence of his country.

1808—Napoleon conquers Spain and places his brother, Joseph, on the throne.

1811 —Venezuela declares independence from Spain on July 5.

1812 —Bolívar conducts his first military campaign, April through July. First Republic of Venezuela falls when Spanish forces enter Caracas on July 28.

1813 —Bolívar returns from exile in New Granada, recaptures Caracas, and declares Second Republic of Venezuela on August 6.

1814 —Napoleon abdicates and goes into exile on April 11. Ferdinand VII regains Spanish throne. Bolívar defeated at Battle of La Puerta and flees to Cartagena.

1815 —Arrives in Jamaica in May, attempts to gain British support. Spanish forces enter Cartagena in December, regaining New Granada.

1816 —Bolívar returns to Venezuela with expeditionary force.

1819 —Congress of Angostura called in January. Bolívar elected president of the Third Republic of Venezuela on February 15. Defeats Spanish forces at Boyacá on August 7. Venezuela and New Granada join as Gran Colombia on December 17.

1821 —Battle of Carabobo ends Spanish occupation of New Granada on June 24. Bolívar returns to Caracas and is declared president of Gran Colombia on June 29.

1822 —Quito (modern Ecuador) falls to Bolívar after Battle of Bomboná and becomes part of Gran Colombia on April 22. Bolívar meets San Martín at Guayaquil on July 26.

1824 —Gains victory at Battle of Junin in August. Last important Spanish Army in Spanish America defeated at Battle of Ayacucho on December 12. Bolívar named dictator of Bolivia.

1826 —Bolívar calls Congress of Panama.

1828 —Assassination attempt on Bolívar in Bogotá on September 25.

1830—Gran Colombia dissolves as Ecuador and Venezuela secede. Bolívar leaves Bogotá on May 8. Dies of tuberculosis on an estate near Santa Marta, Colombia, on December 17.

CHAPTER NOTES

CHAPTER 1. CROSSING THE ANDES

1. Robert J. McNerney, Jr., trans. and ed., *Bolívar and the War for Independence, Memoria del General Daniel Florencio O'Leary* (Austin: University of Texas Press, 1970), pp. 163–64.

2. Salvador de Madariaga, *Bolívar* (New York: Pellegrini and Cudahy, 1952), p. 357.

CHAPTER 2. THE CREOLE MILLIONAIRE

1. Donald E. Worcester, *Bolívar* (Boston: Little, Brown and Company, 1977), p. 9.

2. Salvador de Madariaga, *Bolívar* (New York: Pellegrini and Cudahy, 1952), p. 63.

3. Worcester, p. 8.

4. Robert J. McNerney, Jr., trans. and ed., *Bolívar and the War for Independence, Memoria del General Daniel Florencio O'Leary* (Austin: University of Texas Press, 1970), p. 14.

CHAPTER 3. THE YOUNG REVOLUTIONARY

1. Donald E. Worcester, *Bolívar* (Boston: Little, Brown and Company, 1977), p. 14.

2. Robert J. McNerney, Jr., trans. and ed., *Bolívar and the War for Independence, Memoria del General Daniel Florencio O'Leary* (Austin: University of Texas Press, 1970), p. 16.

3. Lauran Paine, *Bolívar the Liberator* (New York: Roy Publishers, Inc., 1970), p. 24.

4. Worcester, p. 22.

5. Salvador de Madariaga, *Bolívar* (New York: Pellegrini and Cudahy, 1955), p. 116.

6. Ibid., pp. 127–128.

CHAPTER 4. HIS FIRST BATTLE

1. Robert J. McNerney, Jr., trans. and ed., *Bolívar and the War for Independence, Memoria del General Daniel Florencia O'Leary* (Austin: University of Texas Press, 1970), p. 27.

2. Salvador de Madariaga, *Bolívar* (New York: Pellegrini and Cudahy, 1955), p. 165.

3. Ibid., p. 166.

4. Donald E. Worcester, *Bolívar* (Boston: Little, Brown and Company, 1977), p. 29.

5. McNerney, p. 36

6. Worcester, p. 11.

CHAPTER 5. FIRST VICTORIES—AND DEFEAT

1. David Bushnell, ed., *The Liberator, Simón Bolívar—Man and Image* (New York: Alfred A. Knopf, Inc., 1970), p. 5.

2. Donald E. Worcester, *Bolívar* (Boston: Little, Brown and Company, 1977), p. 40.

3. Salvador de Madariaga, *Bolívar* (New York: Pellegrini and Cudahy, 1952), p. 201.

4. Ibid., p. 199.

5. Ibid.

6. Ibid., p. 203.

7. Worcester, pp. 44–45.

8. Madariaga, p. 216.

9. Ibid.

10. Ibid., pp. 224–225.

11. Ibid., 225–226.

12. Ibid., p. 231.

CHAPTER 6. THE FINAL RETURN

1. Donald E. Worcester, *Bolívar* (Boston: Little, Brown and Company, 1977), p. 61.

2. Ibid.

3. Salvador de Madariaga, *Bolívar* (New York: Pellegrini and Cudahy, 1955), pp. 264.

4. Ibid., p. 292.

5. Ibid., p. 286.

CHAPTER 7. THE REPUBLIC OF GRAN COLOMBIA

1. Donald E. Worcester, *Bolívar* (Boston: Little, Brown and Company, 1977), p. 101.

2. Salvador de Madariaga, *Bolívar* (New York: Pellegrini and Cudahy, 1952), p. 393.

3. Ibid., p. 390.

4. Hubert Herring, *A History of Latin America From the Beginnings to the Present* (New York: Alfred A. Knopf, Inc., 1968), p. 282.

5. Madariaga, pp. 440–441.

CHAPTER 8. PLOWING THE SEA

1. Salvador de Madariaga, *Bolívar* (New York: Pellegrini and Cudahy, 1952), p. 482.

2. Ibid., p. 506.

3. Ibid., p. 507.

4. Ibid., p. 533.

5. Donald E. Worcester, *Bolívar* (Boston: Little, Brown and Company, 1977), p. 193.

6. Ibid., p. 571.

7. Ibid., p. 572.

8. Worcester, p. 212.

9. Ibid., pp. 214–215.

10. Ibid., p. 223.

11. Ibid., p. 226.

12. Madariaga, p. 647.

13. David Bushnell, *The Liberator, Simón Bolívar: Man and Image* (New York: Alfred A. Knopf, Inc., 1970), p. 86.

14. Paul Johnson, *The Birth of the Modern* (New York: HarperCollins Publishers, 1991), p. 651.

GLOSSARY

anarchy—A state of society without government or law.

constitutional monarchy—A country ruled by a king or queen whose power is limited by laws.

cortes—The parliament, or congress, of Spain.

Creole—A Spanish citizen born in South America.

intellectual—A person who pursues things of interest to the mind; a student.

junta—A small group that rules a country, especially after the overthrow of a government.

llanero—A person who lives on the northern plains (llanos) of South America centered in Venezuela.

manifesto—A declaration of intentions, objectives, and motives by a person or a political party.

mercenary—A professional soldier serving in a foreign army for pay.

mestizos—South American peoples of mixed European and Indian ancestry.

monarchy—A country that has as head of government a king or queen who has inherited the position.

renegade—A person who deserts a cause, faith, or party for another.

republic—A country that has as the head of government a nominated or elected president, not a king or queen.

royalist—A person who owes allegiance to a king or queen.

secession—The act of withdrawing or resigning from a union or association, usually political.

viceroyalty—A country that has as the head of government a person (viceroy) who is the deputy of a king or queen.

FURTHER READING

Bushnell, David, editor. *The Liberator, Simón Bolívar: Man and Image*. New York: Alfred A. Knopf, Inc., 1970.

Byrnes, Ronald. *Exploring the Developing World: Life in Africa & Latin America*. Denver: University of Denver, Center for Teaching, International Relations Publications, 1993.

García Márquez, Gabriel. *The General in His Labyrinth*. New York: Alfred A. Knopf, Inc., 1990.

Greene, Carol. *Simón Bolívar: South American Liberator*. Chicago: Children's Press, 1989.

Guyatt, John. *Bolivar*. San Diego: Greenhaven Press, Inc., 1980.

Morrison, Marion. *Ecuador, Peru, Bolivia*. Chatham, N.J.: Raintree Steck-Vaughn Publishers, 1992.

Wepman, Dennis. *Simón Bolívar*. New York: Chelsea House Publishers, 1985.

Worcester, Donald E. *Bolívar*. Boston: Little, Brown and Company, 1977.

INDEX

DATE DUE

GAYLORD

PRINTED IN U.S.A.